June 2013

EMPLOYMENT AND TRAINING

Labor's Green Jobs Efforts Highlight Challenges of Targeted Training Programs for Emerging Industries

June 2013

EMPLOYMENT AND TRAINING

Labor's Green Jobs Efforts Highlight Challenges of Targeted Training Programs for Emerging Industries

Why GAO Did This Study

Labor received $500 million from the Recovery Act to help create, better understand, and provide training for jobs within the energy efficiency and renewable energy industries, commonly referred to as "green jobs." Since 2009, Labor has also "greened" existing programs and funded additional green jobs training grants and other efforts.

In light of the amount of funding targeted to green programs within Labor, GAO examined: (1) what is known about the objectives and coordination of Labor's green jobs efforts, (2) what type of green jobs training grantees provided and how selected grantees aligned their training to meet employers' green jobs needs, (3) what is known about program outcomes and what challenges, if any, grantees faced in implementing their programs, and (4) what Labor has done to assist and monitor its green jobs grantees. To conduct this work, GAO reviewed relevant federal laws and regulations; surveyed selected offices within Labor using two questionnaires—one for directly-funded green jobs efforts and one for other efforts; interviewed Labor officials and 11 out of 103 green jobs training grantees; and analyzed relevant Labor documents and data.

What GAO Recommends

GAO recommends that Labor identify lessons learned from the green jobs training programs to enhance its ability to implement such programs in emerging industries. Labor agreed with our recommendation.

View GAO-13-555. For more information, contact Andrew Sherrill at (202) 512-7215 or sherrilla@gao.gov.

What GAO Found

Of the $595 million identified by Labor as having been appropriated or allocated specifically for green jobs activities since 2009, approximately $501 million went toward efforts with training and support services as their primary objective, with much of that funding provided by the American Recovery and Reinvestment Act of 2009 (Recovery Act). Because the Recovery Act directed federal agencies to spend funds quickly and prudently, Labor implemented a number of high-investment green jobs efforts simultaneously. As a result, in some cases, Recovery Act training programs were initiated prior to a full assessment of the demand for green jobs, which presented challenges for grantees. While Labor's internal agencies initially communicated with each other and with other federal agencies after the Recovery Act was passed, most Recovery Act grants have ended or are winding down.

Labor created its green jobs definitional framework to provide local flexibility, and grantees we interviewed broadly interpreted Labor's framework to include any job that could be linked, directly or indirectly, to a beneficial environmental outcome. Labor's training data show most participants were trained in construction or manufacturing. While the findings of our site visits are not generalizable, all grantees we interviewed said they had worked closely with local employers to align their training program with the green skills needs of local employers. Most grantees we interviewed also told us they had incorporated green elements into existing training programs aimed at traditional skills, such as teaching weatherization as part of a carpentry training program.

The outcomes of Labor's green jobs training programs remain uncertain, in part because data on final outcomes were not yet available for about 40 percent of grantees, as of the end of 2012. Analysis of grantees with final outcome data shows they collectively reported training slightly more individuals than they had projected, but job placements were at 55 percent of the target. Training-related job placement rates remain unknown because Labor's Office of Inspector General (OIG) found these data unreliable. Grantees we interviewed were generally positive about Labor's green job training programs, but most said they had faced challenges during implementation, including: (1) a lack of reliable green jobs labor market information, (2) insufficient time to meet grant requirements, (3) knowledge gaps surrounding green skills and changing energy policies, and (4) difficulty placing participants into green jobs, primarily due to the overall poor economy.

Labor has provided technical assistance and taken steps to monitor green jobs training grantees through on-site monitoring visits and quarterly reviews. During these visits and reviews, Labor officials assessed grantee performance, such as by comparing reported program outcomes, including job placements, to targeted performance levels. However, Labor provided only limited guidance on how to document reported job placements. Labor officials required grantees with lower than projected performance levels to implement corrective action plans. In addition, Labor officials told us they have taken steps to improve the quality of grantee reported data, such as by forming an internal workgroup to identify ways to improve the technical assistance they provide to grantees on reporting performance outcomes.

United States Government Accountability Office

Contents

Tables

Figures

Abbreviations

BLS	Bureau of Labor Statistics
CFBNP	Center for Faith-Based and Neighborhood Partnerships
CoP	Community of Practice
EISA	Energy Independence and Security Act of 2007
Energy	Department of Energy
ETA	Employment and Training Administration
ETP	Energy Training Partnership Grants
GCBG	Green Capacity Building Grants
GEMS	Grant Electronic Management System

GGS	Green Goods and Services Survey
GJIF	Green Jobs Innovation Fund
GTP	Green Technologies and Practices Survey
HUD	Department of Housing and Urban Development
HVAC Systems	Heating, Ventilation, and Air Conditioning Systems
ILAB	Bureau of International Labor Affairs
Labor	Department of Labor
MOU	Memorandums of Understanding
MSHA	Mine Safety and Health Administration
OA	Office of Apprenticeship
OASP	Office of the Assistant Secretary for Policy
ODEP	Office of Disability Employment Policy
OFCCP	Office of Federal Contract Compliance Programs
OIG	Officer of the Inspector General
O*NET	Occupational Information Network
OPA	Office of Public Affairs
OSHA	Occupational Safety and Health Administration
OWCP	Office of Workers' Compensation Programs
POP	Pathways Out of Poverty Grants
Recovery Act	American Recovery and Reinvestment Act of 2009
SESP	State Energy Sector Partnership and Training Grants
SLMII	State Labor Market Information Improvement Grants
TA Partnership	Technical Assistance Partnership
UI	Unemployment Insurance
VETS	Veterans' Employment and Training Services
WB	Women's Bureau
WHD	Wage and Hour Division
WIA	Workforce Investment Act of 1998

June 19, 2013

The Honorable Lamar Alexander
Ranking Member
Committee on Health, Education, Labor, and Pensions
United States Senate

The Honorable Michael Enzi
Ranking Member
Subcommittee on Children and Families
Committee on Health, Education, Labor, and Pensions
United States Senate

The American Recovery and Reinvestment Act of 2009 (Recovery Act) provided the Department of Labor (Labor) $500 million in funding aimed at training and placing workers into jobs in the "energy efficiency and renewable energy" industries,[1] commonly referred to as "green jobs." While many of these grants have ended or are currently winding down, they were initiated as part of a strategy aimed at moving the United States toward greater energy independence and security, and green jobs research and training programs were created that were expected to help American workers develop the specialized skills they would need to find and maintain employment in green jobs. Congress passed the framework for this investment—the Green Jobs Act of 2007[2]—more than 5 years ago, and according to Labor officials, funds for green jobs programs were not appropriated until the passage of the Recovery Act in 2009.[3] More recently, Labor has launched a number of efforts to "green" several of its existing programs, and has funded additional green jobs training grants, including the $38 million Green Jobs Innovation Fund (GJIF) grant program. In total, Labor funded 103 green jobs training grantees through the three Recovery Act-funded green jobs training programs and the GJIF

---

[1] See 29 U.S.C. § 2916(e)(1)(B) for a list of these industries.

[2] The Green Jobs Act of 2007, which amended the Workforce Investment Act, was enacted as part of the Energy Independence and Security Act of 2007 (EISA). Pub. L. No. 110-140, 121 Stat. 1492, 1748. EISA concerned, among other things, energy initiatives such as increasing fuel economy standards, increasing the production of biofuels, and improving appliance and lighting standards.

[3] Pub. L. No. 111-5, 123 Stat. 115, 173.

program. In light of the significant amount of funding targeted to green jobs training programs within Labor, this review examines:

1. What is known about the objectives and coordination of Labor's green jobs efforts?

2. What type of green jobs training did grantees provide and how did selected grantees align their training to meet employers' green jobs needs?

3. What is known about program outcomes and what challenges, if any, did grantees face in implementing their programs?

4. What has Labor done to assist and monitor its green jobs grantees?

In addition, the Recovery Act requires that GAO conduct bimonthly reviews of how the act's funds are used by recipients.[4] As part of this review, we examined the use of Recovery Act funds along with other federal funding.

To address the first research question on the objectives and coordination of Labor's green jobs efforts, we compiled an inventory of Labor's green jobs efforts by requesting information from 14 different offices across Labor. These 14 offices were selected based on the likelihood of their administering a green jobs effort or program.[5] We asked these offices to list two separate sets of efforts: (1) efforts where federal funds were appropriated or allocated specifically for green jobs activities and, (2) efforts where federal funds were not specifically appropriated or allocated for green jobs activities, but where the office sought to incorporate green elements into either an existing program or ongoing activity. We gathered additional information on these efforts through two follow-up

---

[4]Pub. L. No. 111-5, § 901, 123 Stat. 115, 191. For a list of our Recovery Act-related products, see http://www.gao.gov/recovery.

[5] For the purposes of this report we refer to organizational entities within Labor as offices. These entities could include agencies, administrations, bureaus, centers, and divisions. Specifically, the 14 offices we identified are: Occupational Safety and Health Administration (OSHA), Mine Safety and Health Administration (MSHA), Women's Bureau (WB), Employment and Training Administration (ETA), Veterans' Employment and Training Services (VETS), Office of the Assistant Secretary for Policy (OASP), Bureau of International Labor Affairs (ILAB), Bureau of Labor Statistics (BLS), Center for Faith-Based and Neighborhood Partnerships (CFBNP), Office of Federal Contract Compliance Programs (OFCCP), Wage and Hour Division (WHD), Office of Workers' Compensation Programs (OWCP), Office of Disability Employment Policy (ODEP), and the Office of Public Affairs (OPA).

questionnaires and received fully completed questionnaires for nearly all efforts.[6]

Because the majority of Recovery Act funding for green jobs efforts was directed toward training programs, we focused much of our review on four grant programs—the three green jobs training programs funded by the Recovery Act (Energy Training Partnership grants, Pathways out of Poverty grants, and State Energy Sector Partnership and Training grants) as well as the newer Green Jobs Innovation Fund. To describe the characteristics of the 103 green jobs training grantees of these four grant programs, we also collected data from the department on the characteristics of green jobs grantees, including grantee location and organizational type.

To better understand the type of green jobs training grantees provided, how grantees aligned their training to meet green jobs needs, and what challenges, if any, they faced in implementing their programs, we interviewed 11 out of the 103 green jobs training grantees and analyzed data provided by Labor. We interviewed grantees in states that had a relatively high number of Labor green jobs grant recipients, states where grantees or sub-grantees received GJIF funds, and states in different geographic regions.[7] During our grantee interviews, we collected information about the types of green jobs training that were funded by Labor's green jobs training grants and the outcomes of grantees' programs, including green job placement. We specifically asked grantees about any challenges they may have encountered as they developed and implemented their program, including whether they experienced challenges placing participants into green jobs. We cannot generalize our findings beyond the interviews we conducted.

---

[6] For the 14 directly-funded green efforts in our scope, we received 13 completed questionnaires and one partially completed questionnaire. We also identified 3 additional directly-funded efforts, for a total of 17 efforts. For the second set of green jobs efforts where funds were not specifically appropriated or allocated for green jobs activities, but where the office sought to incorporate green elements into either an existing program or ongoing activity, we received completed questionnaires for 46 efforts in our scope and we did not survey Labor officials for 2 of the 48 efforts later identified. See appendix I for more information.

[7] We visited grantees in California, Illinois, Minnesota, and Pennsylvania, and interviewed grantees in Connecticut and Louisiana by phone.

To assess the reliability of Labor's data on training type and outcomes, we (1) reviewed existing documentation related to the data sources, including Labor's Office of the Inspector General (OIG) reports, (2) electronically tested the data to identify obvious problems with completeness or accuracy, and (3) interviewed knowledgeable agency officials about the data. We determined that the data were sufficiently reliable for limited purposes. Specifically, we determined that training type data were sufficiently reliable for purposes of reporting out on the types of training most frequently provided by grantees. However, based upon the OIG's findings, we determined that the outcome data were not sufficiently reliable to determine the success of the programs and that data on the extent to which grantees entered training-related employment were not reliable enough to report.

To describe Labor's technical assistance and monitoring efforts, we reviewed technical assistance guides and Labor's Core Monitoring guide, interviewed Labor officials, and discussed Labor's technical assistance with selected grantees. We also obtained and reviewed copies of Labor's monitoring reports for green jobs training grantees. In conducting this review, we also reviewed relevant federal laws, regulations, guidance and pertinent Labor reports and procedures. A more detailed explanation of our scope and methodology can be found in appendix I.

We conducted this performance audit from May 2012 to June 2013 in accordance with generally accepted government auditing standards. Those standards require that we plan and perform the audit to obtain sufficient, appropriate evidence to provide a reasonable basis for our findings and conclusions based on our audit objectives. We believe that the evidence obtained provides a reasonable basis for our findings and conclusions based on our audit objectives.

Background

The Workforce Investment System and Green Jobs Act of 2007

The Department of Labor oversees a number of employment and training programs administered by state and local workforce boards and one-stop career centers established under the Workforce Investment Act of 1998 (WIA). The green jobs training programs Labor has overseen were created under the Green Jobs Act of 2007, which amended WIA. The Green Jobs Act of 2007 was passed as part of the Energy Independence and Security Act of 2007 (EISA),[8] which was intended to move the United States toward greater energy independence and security and to increase the production of clean renewable fuels, among other objectives. This act directed the Secretary of Labor to work in consultation with the Secretary of Energy to create a new worker training program to prepare workers for careers in the energy efficiency and renewable energy industries. However, funds for these programs were not appropriated until the passage of the Recovery Act in 2009, according to Labor officials.

Green Jobs and the Recovery Act

The Recovery Act appropriated $500 million in funding for competitive green jobs grant programs at Labor. The current administration presented the green jobs training grant program as part of a broad national strategy both to create new jobs and to reform how Americans create and consume energy. Specifically, the administration articulated a vision for federal investments in renewable energy to involve coordination across a number of federal agencies to create new, well-paying jobs for Americans and to make such jobs available to all workers.

The Employment and Training Administration (ETA) was responsible for overseeing the implementation of the green jobs training programs that were authorized in the Green Jobs Act of 2007 and funded through the Recovery Act. In June 2009, ETA announced a series of five Recovery Act grant competitions related to green jobs, three of which were primarily focused on training. All of these programs are scheduled to end before the end of July 2013. Table 1 describes these five programs and identifies the types of organizations eligible to receive each grant.

---

[8] Pub. L. No. 110-140, Title X, 121 Stat. 1492, 1748.

Table 1: Green Jobs Grant Programs Funded by the Recovery Act

Program	Description	Eligible grantees	Training focused
Energy Training Partnership (ETP) Grants	Provided funds so grantees could develop partnerships and provide training and supportive services, such as registered apprenticeships, that would lead to employment for individuals in need of updated training and unemployed workers, among others	Private nonprofit organizations that are either national labor-management organizations with local networks or nonprofit partnerships—either statewide or local	Yes
Pathways Out of Poverty (POP) Grants	Provided funds to deliver training and placement services to individuals seeking pathways out of poverty, including unemployed individuals, high school dropouts, individuals with a criminal record, and disadvantaged individuals living in areas of high poverty by providing employment within the energy efficiency and renewable energy sectors	Private nonprofit organizations that deliver services through networks of local affiliates, for example, or whose local affiliates have the ability to provide services in four or more states or public or private local organizations such as community colleges or faith-based organizations	Yes
State Energy Sector Partnership and Training (SESP) Grants	Provided funds for training, job placement, and related activities that reflect a comprehensive energy sector strategy aligned with the governor's overall workforce vision	State workforce investment boards, in partnership with local officials, employer and industry leaders, and labor organizations	Yes
State Labor Market Information Improvement (SLMII) Grants	Provided funds to collect, analyze, and disseminate labor market information and to enhance the labor exchange infrastructure for careers within the energy efficiency and renewable energy sectors	State workforce agencies or consortia of the state workforce agencies of multiple states	No
Green Capacity Building grants (GCBG)	Provided funds to build the capacity of existing Labor grantees to prepare targeted populations for employment in green industries and to support organizations so that they could bolster the capacity of their training programs through the purchase of equipment, staff professional development, curriculum development and/or adaptation, partnership development, and where necessary, the hiring of additional staff	Grantees that had already received a grant from Labor under specified grant programs, such as YouthBuild or Women in Apprenticeship and Non-Traditional Occupations	No

Source: GAO analysis of Labor's Solicitations for Grant Applications.

Between September 2010 and October 2012, Labor's OIG issued a series of three reports related to the department's Recovery Act green jobs programs, including training programs.[9] The most recent report raised questions about the low job placement and retention of trained program participants, the short amount of time for which many participants received training, and limitations of available employment and retention data, among other things.

Labor's Broad Framework for Green Jobs

Labor has used a broad framework to define green jobs, incorporating various elements that have emerged over time as the understanding of what constitutes a green job has evolved. As part of the Green Jobs Act of 2007, WIA was amended to identify seven energy efficiency and renewable energy industries targeted for green jobs training funds.[10] In addition, beginning in 2009, Labor issued information on 12 emerging green sectors as part of a broader effort to describe how the green economy was redefining traditional jobs and the skills required to carry out those jobs.[11] Most recently, in 2010, the Bureau of Labor Statistics (BLS) released a two-part definition of green jobs that was used to count the number of jobs that could be considered green either because what the work produced or how the work was performed benefitted the

[9] U.S. Department of Labor, Office of Inspector General, *Recovery Act: Employment and Training Administration Grant Issuance and Monitoring Policies and Procedures for Discretionary Grants Including Green Jobs Are Comprehensive but Funding Challenges Threaten the Quality of Future Monitoring Activities*, 18-10-013-03-390 (Sept. 30, 2010); *Recovery Act: Slow Pace Placing Workers Into Jobs Jeopardizes Employment Goals of the Green Jobs Program*, 18-11-004-03-390 (Sept. 30, 2011); and *Recovery Act: Green Jobs Program Reports Limited Success in Meeting Employment and Retention Goals as of June 30, 2012*, 18-13-001-03-390 (Oct. 25, 2012).

[10] These seven industries are (1) energy efficient building, construction, and retrofits; (2) renewable electric power; (3) energy efficient and advanced drive train vehicles; (4) biofuels; (5) deconstruction and materials use industries; (6) energy efficiency assessment serving the residential, commercial, or industrial sectors; and (7) manufacturers that produce sustainable products using environmentally sustainable processes and materials.

[11] The Occupational Information Network (O*NET) is overseen by ETA and is the nation's primary source of occupational information. Central to the project is the O*NET database, which contains information on hundreds of standardized and occupation-specific descriptors. O*NET is being developed under the sponsorship of the U.S. Department of Labor's Employment and Training Administration through a grant to the North Carolina Department of Commerce. For more information on O*NET's green economy activities, see http://www.onetcenter.org/green.html.

environment.[12] Figure 1 shows the various elements Labor has used over time to define green jobs.

Figure 1: Key Elements of Labor's Green Framework for Defining Green Jobs

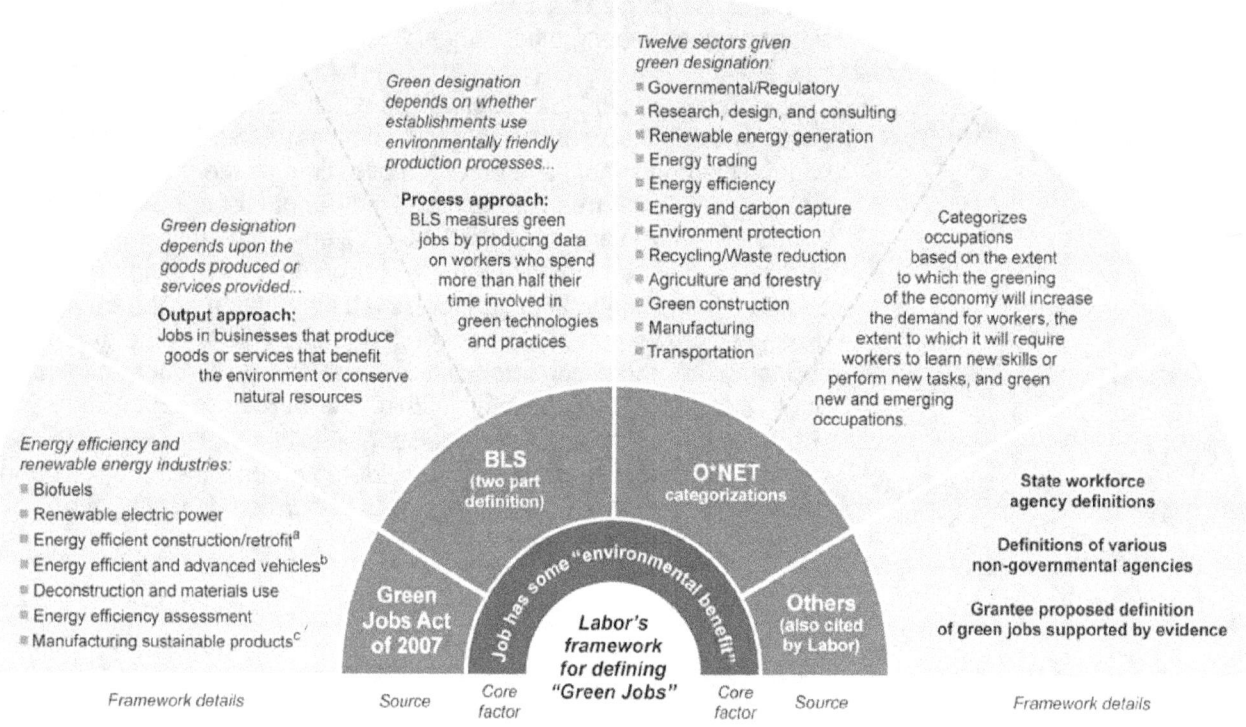

Source: Green Jobs Act of 2007 and GAO review of Labor documents.

[a] Energy efficient building, construction, and retrofit.

[b] Energy efficient and advanced drive train vehicle.

[c] Manufacturers that produce sustainable products using environmentally sustainable processes and materials.

---

[12] According to BLS's definition, green jobs are either (1) jobs in businesses that produce goods or provide services that benefit the environment or conserve natural resources, or (2) jobs in which workers' duties involve making their establishment's production processes more environmentally friendly or use fewer natural resources.

During the implementation of its Recovery Act green jobs training programs and the newer Green Jobs Innovation Fund (GJIF) pilot and demonstration project, which was initiated in 2011 to support job training opportunities for workers in green industry sectors and occupations, Labor has allowed program applicants to use combinations of the various elements to propose the type of training they would provide. For example, Labor permitted grantees of the three Recovery Act-funded programs to develop their green jobs training programs by focusing on training in the seven industries specified by the Green Jobs Act of 2007, or to propose strategies for training in sectors or occupations identified as green within the Occupational Information Network (O*NET). In addition to these two elements, Labor allowed applicants of the more recent GJIF program to use the BLS definition. Furthermore, Labor allowed GJIF applicants to propose their own definition of green jobs if they were able to support their definition with evidence.

Labor Has Focused Its Green Jobs Efforts Largely on Job Training

Most Funding for Green Jobs Efforts Has Been Directed toward Training Workers

According to funding information provided by Labor and our survey of Labor's directly-funded green jobs efforts, most funding for green jobs efforts at Labor has been directed toward programs designed to train individuals for green jobs, with less funding supporting efforts with other objectives, such as data collection or information materials.[13] Indeed, approximately $501 million (84 percent) of the $595 million identified by offices at Labor as having been appropriated or allocated specifically for green jobs activities since 2009 went toward efforts with training and support services as their primary objective.[14] In total, approximately $73 million, or 12 percent of the total amount of funding for green jobs

---

[13] Focus areas generally fell into 1 of 7 categories provided by GAO: (1) information materials; (2) publicity and outreach; (3) technical assistance; (4) partnerships; (5) training and supportive services; (6) data collection and reporting; and (7) capacity building.

[14] We requested information from 14 different offices across Labor. These 14 offices were selected based on the likelihood of their administering a green jobs effort or program.

activities, was reported appropriated or allocated for data collection and reporting efforts.

Most of the funding for green jobs efforts was provided through the Recovery Act, which funded both training and non-training-focused projects at Labor in part to increase energy efficiency and the use of renewable energy sources nationwide. In addition to Recovery Act funding for green jobs efforts, funding information provided by Labor and through our survey of directly-funded green jobs efforts indicate that Labor has allocated at least an additional $89 million since 2009 to support seven other green jobs efforts that have been implemented by five of Labor's offices (see fig. 2). For a brief description of each of Labor's green jobs efforts for which funds were appropriated or allocated, see appendix II.

Figure 2: Funding for Green Jobs Efforts at Labor since 2009, by Office and Focus Area

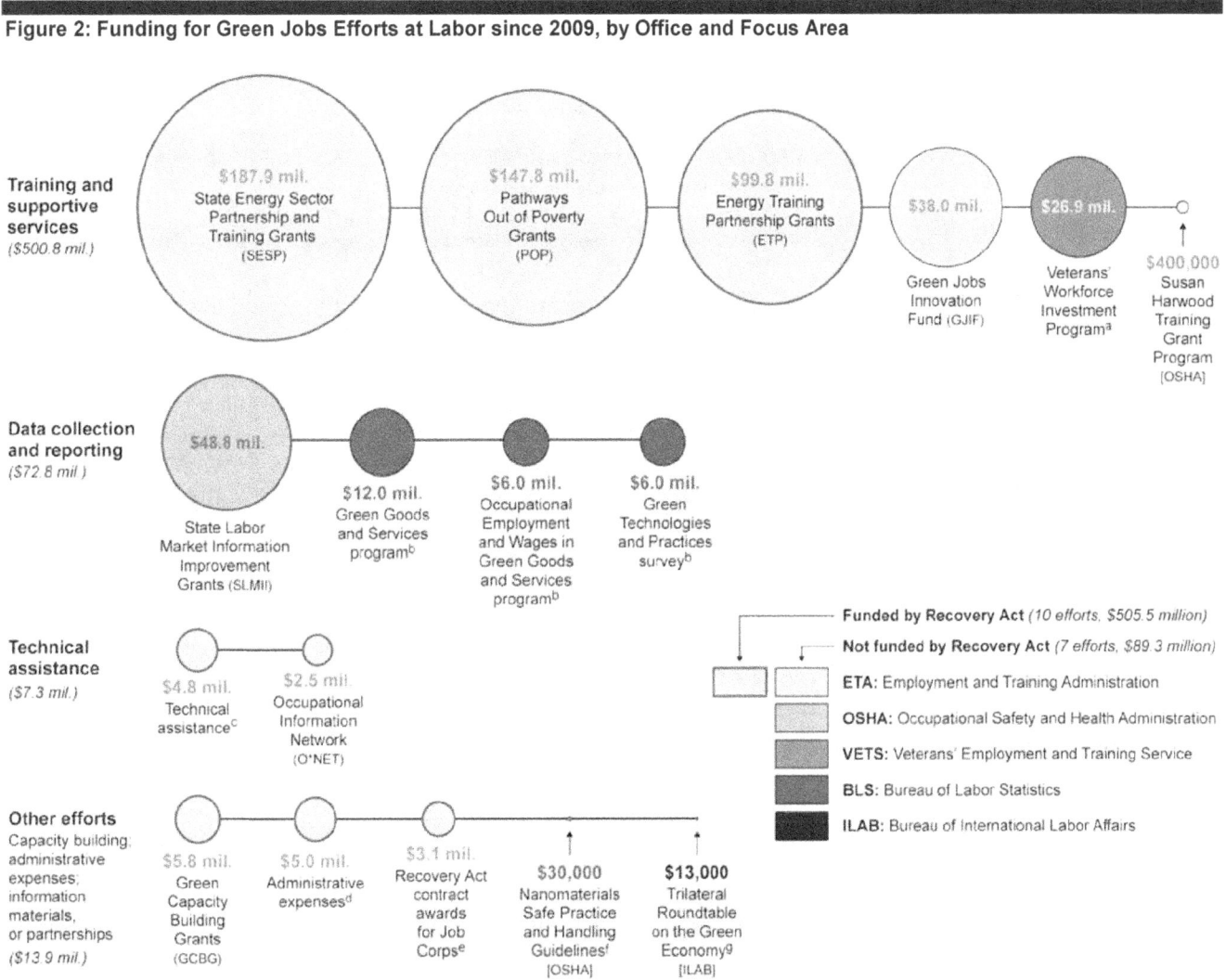

Source: GAO analysis of survey data for directly-funded efforts, funding data provided by Labor, and additional funding identified by GAO.

[a] This figure represents cumulative funding for the program for fiscal years 2009, 2010, and 2011. The amount appropriated or allocated for the program was $7,641,000, $9,641,000, and $9,622,000, respectively.

[b] Since its inception in fiscal year (FY) 2010, through FY 2012, BLS has been appropriated approximately $24 million for the Green Jobs initiative. Of this amount, BLS allocated about $4 million annually for the Quarterly Census of Employment and Wages portion of the Green Goods and Services (GGS) survey; about $2 million annually for the Occupational Employment Statistics portion and; about $2 million annually for the Green Technologies and Practices (GTP) survey. The Employment Projections program was also funded from the same appropriation specifically for green jobs activities.

[c] This figure represents approximately $3.4 million in Recovery Act funding for technical assistance provided through the National Governors Association and its partners for green jobs grantees and approximately $1.5 million in non-Recovery Act funding for technical assistance for GJIF grantees.

Funding for technical assistance for Health Care Sector and Other High Growth and Emerging Industries Grantees is excluded from this funding figure.

^d Administrative expenses include funding for three green jobs evaluations: A Labor Market Information evaluation ($499,980), a Green Jobs and Health Care Implementation Report ($917,248), and a 5-year impact evaluation ($7,992,852).

^e Recovery Act contract awards for Job Corps primarily supported capacity building activities, though some funding was used for training activities.

^f Recovery Act funds were used to fund this effort.

^g Trilateral Roundtable: The Employment Dimension of the Transition to a Green Economy (February 3-4, 2011); this figure represents an expenditure instead of an appropriated or allocated amount.

The Recovery Act directed federal agencies to spend the funds it made available quickly and prudently, and Labor implemented a number of relatively brief but high-investment green jobs efforts simultaneously. As a result, in some cases, Recovery Act training programs were initiated prior to a full assessment of the demand for green jobs.[15] Specifically, Recovery Act-funded green jobs training grantees designed and began to implement their green jobs training programs at the same time states were developing green job definitions and beginning to collect workforce and labor market information on the prevalence and likely growth of green jobs through the State Labor Market Information Improvement grants, which were also funded with Recovery Act funds. Furthermore, BLS launched its Green Jobs initiative—which included various surveys designed to help define and measure the prevalence of green jobs—after many green jobs training programs had begun.[16] ETA officials noted that BLS's development of the definition of green jobs was a deliberative and extensive process that required consulting stakeholders and the public. They also said that BLS's timeline for defining green jobs differed from ETA's timeline for awarding and executing grants, which was driven by Recovery Act mandates.

Labor has made subsequent investments that build upon lessons learned through the Recovery Act grant programs. For example, ETA initiated the $38 million GJIF program in 2011 to support job training opportunities for workers in green industry sectors and occupations. In developing the GJIF grant program, ETA considered lessons learned through the

---

[15] Labor provided extensions to the original period of performance for selected grantees in each of the five Recovery Act green jobs grant programs (see fig. 3).

[16] According to Labor officials, the BLS Green Jobs initiative was not connected to the Recovery Act in any way.

Recovery Act grant programs.[17] For example, various stakeholders including employers, the public workforce system, federal agencies, and foundations identified Registered Apprenticeship—training that combines job related technical instruction with structured on-the-job learning experiences for skilled trades and allows participants to earn wages—as a valuable workforce strategy. ETA acknowledged that upgrading basic skills, including literacy and math, is critical to ensure job placement and suggested that training participants exclusively in green skills is not always sufficient. Consequently, ETA required GJIF grantees to implement green jobs training programs that would either forge linkages between Registered Apprenticeship and pre-apprenticeship programs or deliver integrated basic skills and occupational training through community-based organizations. Figure 3 shows a timeline illustrating the rollout of selected green jobs grants at Labor and the time periods during which these grants were active,[18] as well as the timing of BLS's efforts to collect data on green jobs. With the exception of the GJIF grants, all of these efforts will have been completed by July 2013.

---

[17] This grant is included in the $89 million identified by Labor as allocated or appropriated for green jobs activities in addition to the Recovery Act-funded programs (see fig. 2).

[18] ETA refers to this time as the period of performance.

Figure 3: Timeline of Selected Green Jobs Efforts at Labor

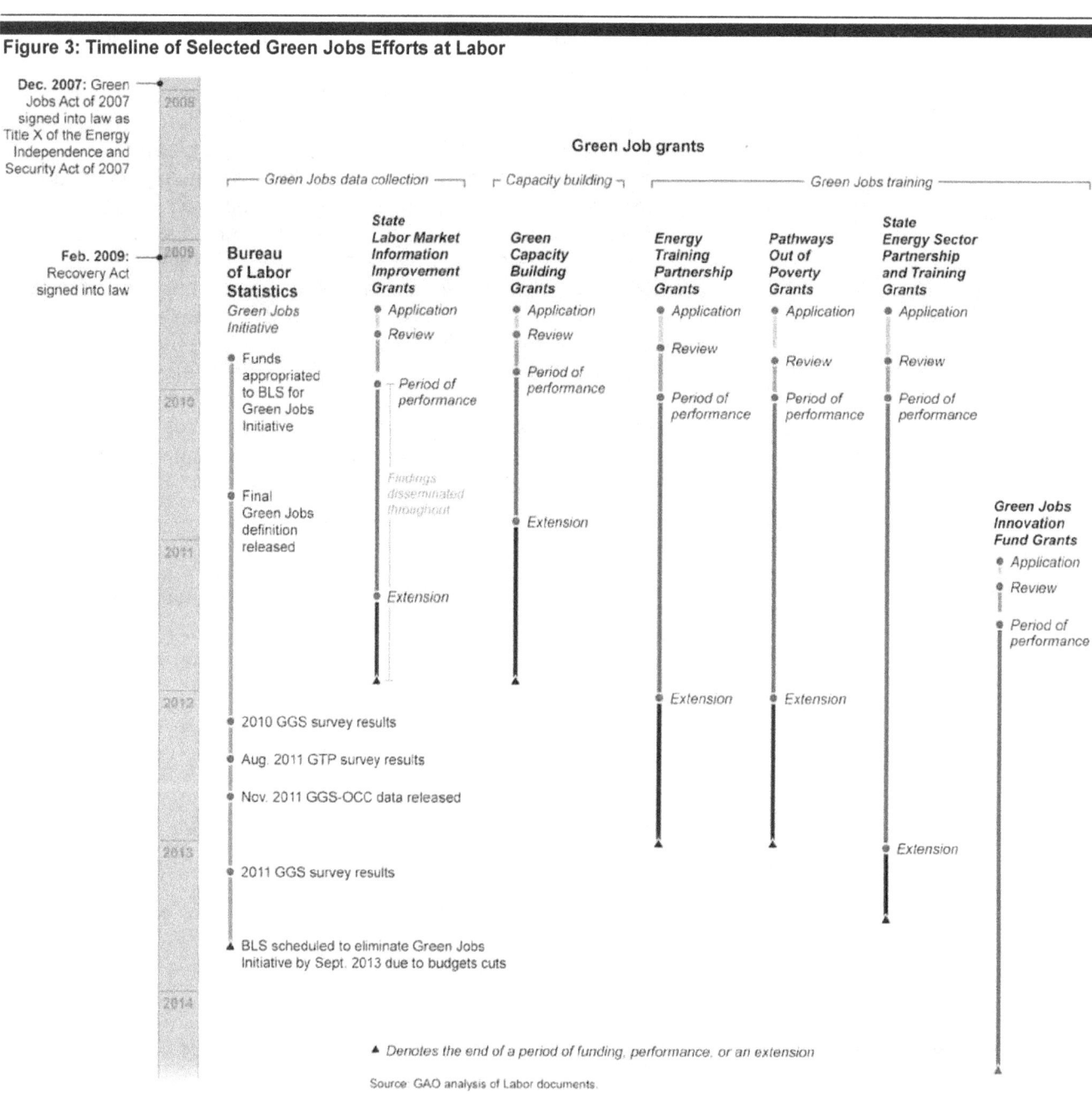

Dec. 2007: Green Jobs Act of 2007 signed into law as Title X of the Energy Independence and Security Act of 2007

Feb. 2009: Recovery Act signed into law

Green Job grants

— Green Jobs data collection — ┌ Capacity building ┐ ┌— Green Jobs training —┐

Bureau of Labor Statistics
Green Jobs Initiative
- Funds appropriated to BLS for Green Jobs Initiative
- Final Green Jobs definition released
- 2010 GGS survey results
- Aug. 2011 GTP survey results
- Nov. 2011 GGS-OCC data released
- 2011 GGS survey results
- ▲ BLS scheduled to eliminate Green Jobs Initiative by Sept. 2013 due to budgets cuts

State Labor Market Information Improvement Grants
- Application
- Review
- Period of performance
- *Findings disseminated throughout*
- Extension

Green Capacity Building Grants
- Application
- Review
- Period of performance
- Extension

Energy Training Partnership Grants
- Application
- Review
- Period of performance
- Extension

Pathways Out of Poverty Grants
- Application
- Review
- Period of performance
- Extension

State Energy Sector Partnership and Training Grants
- Application
- Review
- Period of performance

Green Jobs Innovation Fund Grants
- Application
- Review
- Period of performance
- Extension

▲ Denotes the end of a period of funding, performance, or an extension

Source: GAO analysis of Labor documents.

Distribution and Characteristics of Green Jobs Training Grantees

Grantees from all but six states received at least one of the 103 green jobs training grants that were awarded by ETA,[19],[20] but grantees were somewhat concentrated within certain regions of the country. Specifically, most states with three or more grantees were located in the Northeast, West, or Midwest regions of the country.[21] Four states and the District of Columbia received five or more green jobs training grants: California, Michigan, New York, and Pennsylvania. Figure 4 shows the number of green jobs training grants awarded by state.

---

[19] In total, ETA awarded 189 green jobs grants with Recovery Act funding, of which 97 were primarily focused on training. In addition, ETA awarded 6 GJIF training grants for green jobs training. The analysis in this section pertains to the 103 training specific green jobs grants awarded through the 3 Recovery Act-funded programs primarily focused on training (SESP, POP, and ETP) and the GJIF program, which was funded as a pilot and demonstration project under WIA.

[20] Over half of grantees provided training through a network of local affiliates or sub-affiliates, sometimes within a single state or located in multiple states. Labor officials could not provide the exact number or location of such sub-grantees for the three Recovery Act-funded green jobs training programs, so this analysis includes only the location of primary grant recipients.

[21] As defined by the U.S. Census Bureau.

Figure 4: Green Jobs Training Grantees, by State

Source: GAO analysis of Labor data

In terms of organizational type, most green jobs training grants were awarded to nonprofit organizations and state workforce agencies (see fig. 5). Specifically, 44 percent of green jobs training grants were awarded to nonprofit organizations and 34 percent were awarded to state governmental agencies or departments. In addition, 10 percent of grantees were organized labor or labor management organizations. ETA officials from all six of its regional offices said that in terms of organizational type, green jobs training grantees did not differ substantially from the types of grantees ETA typically oversees. ETA officials said building partnerships had been an important focus of the green jobs grants, and indeed ETA's grant solicitations required, or in some cases encouraged, grant recipients, regardless of organizational type, to develop partnerships with various stakeholders, such as representatives of the workforce system, industry groups, employers, unions, the education and training community, nonprofits, or community-based organizations. Staff from ETA's regional offices said that some grantees developed new and successful partnerships as a result of the grants, including partnerships with labor unions.

Figure 5: Green Jobs Training Grantees, by Organizational Type

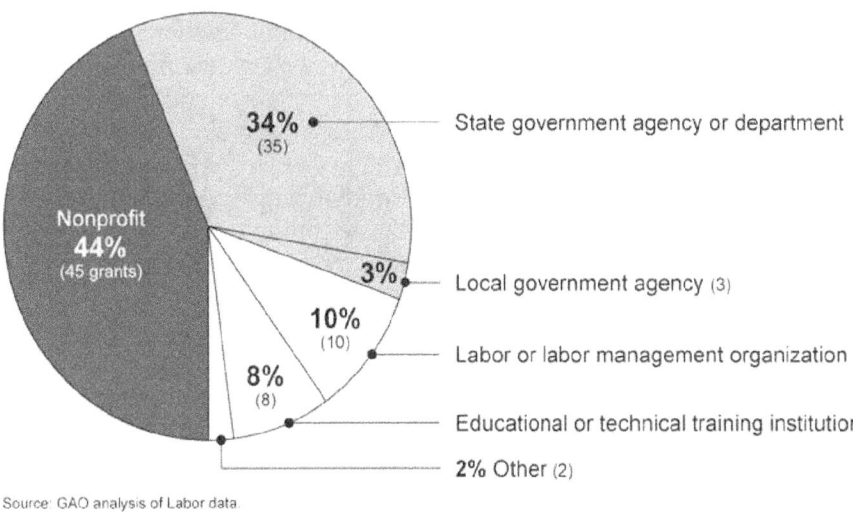

State government agency or department — 34% (35)

Nonprofit 44% (45 grants)

Local government agency (3) — 3%

Labor or labor management organization — 10% (10)

Educational or technical training institution — 8% (8)

2% Other (2)

Source: GAO analysis of Labor data

More than half of ETA's green jobs training grantees implemented their grants through sub-grantees, or a network of local affiliates, rather than providing training services directly to participants. Grantees that contract with sub-grantees or local affiliates to provide services are responsible for monitoring and overseeing how all grant funds are used, effectively delegating day-to-day oversight responsibility from Labor to the primary grantee.[22]

Labor's Efforts to Infuse Green Jobs into Existing Programs

In addition to Labor's direct investments in green jobs, several offices at Labor have infused green elements into their ongoing activities even though funds were not specifically appropriated or allocated for these green jobs efforts. In total, of the 14 Labor offices we surveyed, 6 identified and implemented 48 such efforts (for a list of the efforts, see appendix III). Some of these offices added a "layer of green" to existing training programs or other activities. For example, according to material provided by Labor, most YouthBuild programs have incorporated green building into their construction training. Other efforts focused on providing

---

[22] Labor provides oversight of sub-grantees through its monitoring of primary grantees, which includes ensuring that primary grantees monitor their sub-grantees and document monitoring results.

information materials, forming partnerships, or conducting publicity and outreach, among other things. For example, the Women's Bureau[23] created a guide on sustainable careers for women and Labor's Occupational Safety and Health Administration contributed to an Environmental Protection Agency publication on best practices for improving indoor air quality during home energy upgrades. Further, in 2010 the Center for Faith-Based and Neighborhood Partnerships hosted a roundtable discussion about green jobs between the Secretary of Labor and leaders from national foundations and discussed how to create employment opportunities for low-income populations in the green jobs industry.

Several of Labor's Offices Coordinate on Implementing Green Jobs Efforts within Labor or with Other Federal Agencies

Although funding for green jobs efforts at Labor has shifted and green jobs efforts funded through the Recovery Act are winding down, a few of Labor's ongoing programs or efforts continue to emphasize green jobs or skills, and Labor continues to incorporate green elements into existing programs by coordinating internally on an as-needed basis. After the passage of the Recovery Act, a number of Labor's offices worked together to implement the requirements of the act, and Labor officials said that they collaborated on green jobs efforts on a fairly regular basis and that more formal green jobs meetings across the department were common. For those green jobs efforts where green elements have been infused into ongoing activities even though funds were not specifically appropriated or allocated for green jobs efforts, offices at Labor indicated through our survey that they continue to coordinate on such efforts within Labor and across other federal agencies, albeit in a less formal manner. For example, according to our survey of these indirectly-funded green jobs efforts, for 37 of 46 of the efforts listed in appendix III, offices said that they coordinated with others at Labor, and for 30 of 46 of the efforts, they reported coordinating with other federal agencies.[24] In addition, it is likely that coordination on green jobs efforts will continue to occur on an ad-hoc basis, especially as funding and priorities within the department

---

[23] Ensuring that green jobs would be accessible to women and minorities was identified as a significant challenge in the Vice President's 2009 Middle Class Task Force report, *Green Jobs: a Pathway to a Strong Middle Class.*

[24] While there are 48 efforts in total, we did not survey Labor officials for 2 of the 48 efforts listed in appendix III.

shift. For example, Labor recently reported that due to federal budget cuts, BLS has discontinued its reporting on employment in green jobs.

According to a Labor official, after the Recovery Act was passed, Labor collaborated with other departments, such as the Department of Energy (Energy) and the Department of Housing and Urban Development (HUD) to foster job growth for a new green economy. For example, Labor's Occupational Safety and Health Administration worked with Energy on retrofitting and safety activities, and Labor also partnered with HUD to provide green jobs training and possible employment opportunities to public housing residents. In addition, Labor entered into various Memorandums of Understanding (MOU) after the Recovery Act was passed to collaborate on green jobs-related issues with other federal agencies. For example, the Secretaries of Energy, Labor, and the Department of Education announced a collaboration to connect jobs to training programs and career pathways and to make cross-agency communication a priority. While these examples highlight coordination on green jobs efforts after the passage of the Recovery Act, little is known about the effectiveness of these efforts.

Selected Grantees Broadly Defined Green Jobs and Generally Added Green Elements to Existing Training Programs

To identify the potential demand for green jobs in their communities, all (11 of 11)[25] grantees we interviewed had broadly interpreted Labor's green jobs definitional framework to include as green any job that could be linked, directly or indirectly, to a beneficial environmental outcome. While Labor created its framework to provide local flexibility, the wide variation in the types of green jobs obtained by program participants illustrates just how broadly Labor's definition can be interpreted and raises questions about what constitutes a green job—especially in cases where the job essentially takes the form of a more traditional job (see table 2). In general, grantees we interviewed considered jobs green if they could link the job to (1) a green industry, (2) the production or installation of goods that benefit the environment, (3) the performance of services that potentially lead to environmental benefits, or (4) environmentally beneficial work processes. For example, in some cases, grantees we interviewed considered jobs green because they were linked

---

[25] The number of grantees interviewed and training programs examined totaled 11. Therefore, for the remainder of this section, only the relevant count of grantees or programs will be presented within parentheses and it can be assumed that the count is out of 11. It can also be assumed that the qualifier "all" equates to 11.

to the renewable energy industry, such as solar panel installation or sales. Grantees considered other jobs green because the goods being produced benefited the environment, such as the pouring of concrete for a wind turbine or the installation of energy efficient appliances. In some cases the green job was service-based, such as an energy auditor or energy surveyor. Finally, other grantees considered jobs green because of the environmentally beneficial processes being used, such as applying paint in an efficient manner or using advanced manufacturing techniques that reduce waste. Even for jobs where parts of the work have a link to environmentally beneficial outcomes, workers may only use green skills or practices for a portion of the time they work. For instance, technicians trained to install and repair high-efficiency heating, ventilation, and air conditioning (HVAC) systems may in the course of their work also install less energy efficient equipment.[26]

[26] BLS counts a job as being green if it is held by a worker who spends over half their time involved in green technologies and practices.

Table 2: Examples of Green Job Placement Based on Interviews with Selected Labor Green Jobs Grantees

Training focus	Green job placement examples
Renewable energy	• solar panel installer • solar panel sales representative
Green construction and retrofitting	• construction laborer building an energy efficient home • laborer inspecting and weatherizing homes • operator driving heavy machinery on a public rail project • concrete pourer on a wind-turbine project site • plumber installing low-flow toilets and water saving fixtures • hardwood floor layer installing sustainable flooring materials • worker trained to apply paint in a manner that reduces waste and toxic emissions
Electrical work	• electrician installing energy-efficient lighting controls • maintenance advisor on energy-saving appliances and lighting alternatives for property managers
Heating, Ventilation, and Air Conditioning (HVAC) Systems	• HVAC technician installing high-efficiency furnaces and air conditioning units • worker who conducts energy surveys to educate building owners on cost-effective energy efficiency alternatives • maintenance technician overseeing compliance on EPA emission regulations
General and hazardous waste management	• laborer on an environmental clean-up project • laborer removing hazardous waste from a factory site
Manufacturing	• factory line-worker trained to identify opportunities to reduce waste • machinist using computerized technology that reduces waste
Other	• emergency medical technician trained to perform rescues on wind turbine towers

Source: GAO analysis of information from selected Labor green jobs training grantees.

All grantees we interviewed said they had worked closely with local employers to align their training program with the green skills needs of local employers. All agreed developing effective relationships with employers was crucial to aligning any training program with available jobs.[27] Labor's three Recovery Act green jobs training programs, as well

---

[27] Labor has asserted the importance of the involvement of local employers in the alignment of employment training programs with jobs. For example, WIA requires that a majority of local workforce investment boards be representatives of local businesses. GAO has also reported on the importance of linking the workforce investment system with employers to meet local labor market needs. See GAO, *Workforce Investment Act: Innovative Collaborations between Workforce Boards and Employers Helped Meet Local Needs*, GAO-12-97 (Washington, D.C. Jan. 19, 2012).

as the GJIF program, all required applicants to demonstrate how they would partner with local employers to develop and implement their training programs. Most (9) grantees told us they had assembled advisory boards consisting of representatives from local businesses and industry associations to help inform them about available green jobs and the skills that would most likely be in demand by local employers. Further, all grantees said they engaged in ongoing communication with employers to stay abreast of changes in the local economy and employer needs, and most (10) made changes to their program curricula or tailored their training in response to employer input.

Labor's data show that green jobs training grantees primarily offered training in the construction and manufacturing industries. Specifically, nearly half of all participants of the Recovery Act-funded green jobs training programs received training focused on construction, and approximately 15 percent received training in manufacturing. Over 5 percent of participants in those programs received training in other industries that included utilities, transportation, and warehousing. Grantees in Labor's newer GJIF program focused even more heavily on construction—approximately 94 percent of participants were trained in construction and around 3 percent in manufacturing.

Most grantees (9) we spoke to had infused green elements into existing training curricula for more traditional skills. However, the extent to which the training focused on green versus traditional skills varied across programs and often depended upon the skill level of targeted participants. Most (7) of the programs we visited generally targeted relatively low-skilled individuals with limited work experience and were designed to teach participants the foundational skills they would need to pursue a career in a skilled trade in which green skills and materials can be used. For example, those programs typically used their green job grant funds to incorporate green skills into existing construction, carpentry, heating/air-conditioning, plumbing, or electricity programs. The programs generally involved a mixture of classroom and hands-on training and taught traditional skills, such as how to read blueprints, use tools, install and service appliances, and frame buildings. In teaching these skills, however, instructors also showed students the way the processes or products used in performing these tasks could lead to environmentally beneficial outcomes. For example, participants were taught various ways to weatherize a building to conserve energy, to efficiently operate heavy machines to save fuel, or to install solar panels as part of a green construction project.

In contrast, two programs we visited focused more exclusively on short-term green skills training to supplement the existing traditional skills of relatively higher-skilled unemployed workers. For example, one green awareness program taught participants to identify ways to perform their work, such as manufacturing, in a more environmentally beneficial manner, often by identifying and reducing waste. Another program added a component to their comprehensive electrical training program to train unemployed registered electricians how to install and maintain advanced energy efficient lighting systems. The grantees associated with both of these programs, as well as other grantees, noted that employer demand for workers with green skills may sometimes be most effectively met through short-term training of higher-skilled unemployed workers or incumbent workers.

Outcomes of Green Jobs Training Remain Uncertain, with Grantees Citing Implementation Challenges

Outcomes of Green Jobs Training Programs Remain Largely Unknown Due to Data Lags

The overall impact of Labor's green jobs training programs remains largely uncertain partly because some individuals are still participating in training and are not expected to have outcomes yet, and because final outcome data are submitted to Labor approximately 3 months after the grant period ends.[28] The most recent performance outcome data for the three Recovery Act-funded and GJIF green jobs grants are as of December 31, 2012, at which time approximately 60 percent of the Recovery Act-funded programs had ended and grantees had submitted final performance outcome data. According to Labor officials, complete outcome data for the remaining Recovery Act-funded green jobs grantees will likely not be available until October 2013 because many grants were

---

[28] Labor officials told us that these time frames are based on grantee performance reporting requirements.

extended to June 2013. They also said that final performance outcome data for the GJIF grant—which is scheduled to end in June 2014—will likely not be available until October 2014. Our analysis of data reported by Recovery Act-funded green jobs grantees with final outcome data shows that these grantees collectively reported enrolling and training more participants than they had proposed when setting their outcome targets.[29] However, their placement of program participants into employment lagged in comparison—these grantees reported placing 55 percent of the projected number of participants into jobs. When final data become available for the remaining 40 percent of grantees, the final figure comparing reported employment outcomes to proposed targets may change.[30] Moreover, it remains to be seen how GJIF grantees' employment outcomes will compare to their projected targets, and whether the employment outcomes of this program will benefit either from economic changes or lessons learned since the Recovery Act programs began.

Developing a complete and accurate assessment of Labor's green jobs training programs is further challenged by the potential unreliability of certain outcome data—particularly for placement into training-related employment. In its October 2012 report, Labor's OIG questioned the reliability of the Recovery Act green jobs training programs' employment and retention outcome data because a significant proportion of sampled data for employment and retention outcomes were not adequately

---

[29] Collectively for these grantees, the number of program participants enrolled was 104 percent of the grantees' aggregate target level, and the number of program participants completing training was 106 percent of the grantees' aggregate target level.

[30] This analysis of reported outcome data only includes grantees in two of the three Recovery-Act funded green jobs training programs because final outcome data were not available for any grantees of the third program. Specifically, all grantees that had reported final outcome data as of December 31, 2012, were either Pathways Out of Poverty grantees or Energy Training Partnership grantees. Almost all grantees for which final outcome data had not yet been reported were grant recipients of the State Energy Sector and Partnership and Training (SESP) grants. Employment-placement outcomes and earnings might vary systematically across grant programs due to differences in the populations targeted by the grants. For example, Pathways Out of Poverty grantees served unemployed individuals, high school dropouts, and other disadvantaged individuals within areas of high poverty. In contrast, under SESP grants, various target populations were given priority to receive training, such as workers impacted by national energy and environmental policy, veterans, and unemployed individuals, among other groups. Other individuals, such as entry-level and incumbent workers were also eligible to be served through the SESP program.

supported by grantee documentation.[31] We reviewed the OIG's data review process and found it appropriate for assessing reliability and therefore also consider the data unreliable for evaluating program performance.[32] While outcome data for the ongoing GJIF program are still being reported and the OIG did not assess the reliability of this program's data, Labor's method for collecting these data remains largely unchanged from that used for the Recovery Act-funded green jobs training programs. Consequently, these outcome data—particularly for placement into training-related employment—could also be questionable.

Labor officials noted that they have been collecting additional information on employment outcomes and wages using state unemployment insurance (UI) wage record data on program participants, and will continue to do so into early 2015 for the GJIF program.[33] Results of their most recent analyses of UI data showed that, of the participants who had exited at least one of the three Recovery Act-funded green jobs training programs between April 1, 2011, and March 31, 2012, 52 percent had obtained employment.[34] Similar analyses provided by Labor showed that, of participants who had exited between October 1, 2010, and September 30, 2011, 83 percent of those who had become employed had retained their employment for at least 6 months and had average earnings of

---

[31] For their data reliability assessment, Labor's OIG performed a file review of outcome data for eight randomly selected grantees of the Recovery Act programs. They found that 24 percent of entered employment outcomes were not supported by adequate documentation, and that 33 percent of training-related entered employment outcomes were not supported by adequate documentation. Most of the documentation problems were found with three of the eight sampled grantees.

[32] For a complete description of our data reliability assessment process, see appendix I.

[33] GAO previously reported that UI wage records provide a fairly consistent national view of the performance of WIA. The report noted that most of the outcome data reported in a given program year actually reflect participants who left the program during the prior year, which limits their usefulness for gauging current program performance. GAO has not recently assessed how Labor calculates entered employment rates, job retention rates, or average earnings using these data. See: GAO, *Workforce Investment Act: States and Local Areas Have Developed Strategies to Assess Performance, but Labor Could Do More to Help,* GAO-04-657, (Washington, D.C.: June 1, 2004).

[34] According to Labor, their most recent analyses of Recovery Act green jobs training program outcomes using UI wage data are based on data as of December 31, 2012. The data contain employment information for program participants who had exited training during the one-year period ending March 31, 2012. The data contain job retention and earnings information for program participants who had exited training during the one-year period ending September 30, 2011.

around $25,000 for the 6 month period. Results of Labor's analysis of UI wage data for participants of the GJIF program shows that 40 percent of participants who had exited between April 1, 2011, and March 31, 2012, had entered employment.[35] However, the UI data do not capture whether jobs obtained were training-related for either the Recovery Act-funded or GJIF programs, so, absent additional relevant information, the extent to which grantees placed participants into training-related employment may never be reliably known.

According to Labor officials, once complete, these additional UI wage data may provide more definitive information on the extent to which program participants entered employment and will be used by the department to develop a broader picture of the grant programs' level of success in achieving employment outcomes. Specifically, Labor officials said that while there is not a formal process to study the UI data, program staff routinely examine these data to identify lessons learned and best practices that could be applied to future grant programs. Labor officials said the data could be used to compare the green jobs training programs against other training programs across the agency, such as those under WIA, if resources permit. While Labor officials consider the UI data to be more definitive than the grantee-reported job placement data to measure overall program outcomes once the grant period ends, they stressed the importance of having real-time data to monitor grantee performance during implementation.

While the UI wage record data provide an alternative source of information on job placement outcomes, due to a 9-month lag time, these data are of limited usefulness regarding program management. Specifically, because of the time lag, grantees could not use these data to monitor their progress toward meeting program goals in real-time. Further, Labor could not use the data to hold grantees accountable for meeting grant goals, as all grant periods will have ended before the data are complete. Consequently, ensuring the reliability of grantee reported outcome data remains vitally important, particularly for grant programs

---

[35] According to Labor, their most recent analyses of the GJIF green jobs training program outcomes using UI wage data are based on data as of December 31, 2012. The data contain employment information for program participants who had exited training during the one-year period ending March 31, 2012. Also according to Labor, relevant UI wage data to generate job retention rates or average earnings for participants of the GJIF program are not yet available.

whose primary objective is to prepare workers for attaining employment in a targeted emerging industry.

Grantees Highlighted Green Jobs Training Benefits and Challenges

The grantees we interviewed were generally positive about Labor's green jobs training programs, with most speaking optimistically about the potential value of the green skills obtained by the program participants. Most grantees we met with said that they believe there to be a continued national movement towards lowering energy usage—whether due to economic, policy, or cultural changes[36]—and all projected that the demand for workers with green skills credentials will continue to rise. All (11 of 11) were of the opinion that possessing green skills in addition to more traditional skills provides workers with an advantage as they seek a new job or move along a career pathway, and most (10) cited the need for training programs that provide nationally or industry-recognized green credentials. Two noted that having multiple credentials was particularly valuable. Lastly, some (5) grantees mentioned that the benefits of the green jobs training, like most job training, may not become apparent immediately, but may often be realized later during the worker's career, especially as demand for green skills grows.

However, all grantees noted there have been challenges associated with developing and implementing Labor's green jobs training programs. For example, most (8) of the grantees we interviewed said that the lack of credible green jobs labor market information had limited their ability to identify or predict the level of available green jobs or the demand for green skills in their local area. Although state workforce agencies received funding to conduct green jobs labor market information studies under the State Labor Market Information Improvement grants, most resulting data were issued after many Recovery Act training programs had already begun. In addition, the BLS surveys were released from March 2012 through March 2013, after GJIF grantees had submitted their applications outlining their training programs to Labor. Having access to

---

[36] All 11 grantees we interviewed were of the opinion there is a national movement toward energy efficiency due to economic changes, whereby industries or singular businesses are attempting to be globally competitive partly by reducing energy costs. Ten of the grantees were also of the opinion that such a national movement is also being driven by policy changes, such as state energy goals, and by cultural changes, such as public concern about global warming or public desire for U.S. energy independence. One grantee was not of the opinion that such a national movement was being driven by policy or cultural changes.

GAO-13-555 Employment and Training

the final results of the state labor market information studies could have provided Recovery Act grantees with additional insights into their state's economic activity in the energy efficiency and renewable energy industries, as well as jobs within those industries when they were developing their training programs. Similarly, BLS survey results could have provided GJIF grantees with a national snapshot of establishments that produce green goods and services and the jobs of workers involved in green activities, among other information, and may have provided grantees with additional context for the development and implementation of their green jobs training programs.[37] Labor officials said the rapidly evolving nature of the green industries has resulted in multiple changes to employer green job demand information over the course of the grant periods, further complicating their attempts to provide labor market information for this sector.

In addition, most (9) grantees we met with said Labor's green jobs training grants did not afford them enough time to both develop local partnerships and recruit, train, and place program participants. All grantees said developing partnerships can be especially time-consuming if such partnerships had not existed prior to the grant award.[38] Most (9) noted that given how important local partnerships are to developing successful training programs, training programs that require such partnerships should have longer grant periods than those afforded by the Recovery Act and GJIF programs.

Furthermore, most (8) grantees mentioned how developing and implementing a relatively new type of training, like green skills, can require additional time in order to fill knowledge gaps among employers. This may be especially true in light of changing state and local energy policies. For example, according to the Department of Energy, as of March 2013, 29 states have established standards aimed at generating a

---

[37] The three surveys launched by BLS are (1) the 2010 and 2011 Green Goods and Services (GGS) surveys; (2) the Green Technologies and Practices (GTP) survey; and (3) the Occupational Employment and Wages in Green Goods and Services (GGS-OCC) program.

[38]U.S. Department of Labor, *Green Jobs and Health Care Implementation Study Final Report* (Sept. 20, 2012), noted that using pre-existing partner relationships contributed to the efficiency of program implementation. Further, the report suggested that requiring future grant administrators to identify partners with whom they have had positive pre-existing relationships would likely limit the amount of up-front administrative time spent working with partners—especially for grants with shorter periods of performance.

certain percentage of the state's energy using renewable sources by a specified year. Furthermore, many municipalities throughout the country are requiring that local construction projects adhere to environmentally friendly requirements. However, most (9) grantees we spoke with said some employers may not recognize how changing policies will affect their businesses. In fact, they believe this lack of understanding may be limiting demand for workers trained in green skills. To address this problem, one of the grantees we interviewed had developed a 1-day training program for local business managers to educate them about how they could benefit from the green skills that participants were obtaining through the organization's training program. Most (6) grantees said at times during the implementation of their green jobs training program, they were, in effect, attempting to simultaneously drive both supply and demand for workers with green skills, which took considerable time and effort.

In addition, although all grantees we interviewed had engaged with employers who had committed their support for the training curriculum, they also said this did not always translate into green jobs for program participants. Above all, most (9) pointed to the slow economic recovery as the reason their predictions—and those made by employers—regarding green job growth were not fully realized. For example, one grantee explained how the local housing market had not recovered as quickly as anticipated, and as a result, demand for workers with green skills—such as green construction techniques, weatherization practices, and the installation of energy efficient appliances—has been sluggish. In addition, most (10) grantees explained that because green skills are often intertwined with traditional skills training and the skilled labor industries, their programs' participants were negatively affected by the overall poor economy. For example, most grantees (9) noted how their program participants, despite their additional layer of green skills training, found themselves competing with a high number of unemployed workers who were also seeking to regain employment in more traditional jobs such as carpentry or electrical work. Most (9) grantees also noted that renewable energy sectors, such as solar power, have not grown in their regions as was predicted several years ago. Lastly, most (7) grantees we interviewed said it is difficult to accurately measure the value of green skills training in terms of green job placement. In general, they said this is partly because, unlike jobs in other growing industries, like health care, there are few distinctly green jobs. One grantee we met with said she believes the term "green job" is misleading, and complicates program implementation. This grant official said that funding should be directed toward supplementing traditional skills training with green skills that can be used on any job rather than on preparing workers for specific jobs identified as green.

Based on our interviews with grantees of Labor's green jobs training programs, and the descriptions of their experiences implementing those programs, we identified several lessons learned that may warrant consideration when implementing similar targeted grant programs for other emerging industries (see table 3).

Table 3: Lessons Learned Associated with Implementing Grant Programs for an Emerging Industry

Implementing grant programs for an emerging industry may require…	Lessons learned based on selected grantees' experiences implementing Labor's green jobs training programs
…a more nimble approach	• Setting realistic outcome goals can be complicated by uncertainty regarding the economy and public policies. • If available labor market information is limited, significant, ongoing employer involvement will likely be required. • Local market conditions may quickly change necessitating modifications to training and grant agreements. • There can be unanticipated challenges to training and placing target populations into jobs as the industry continues to evolve.
… longer grant periods	• Building effective relationships with employers and key partners can require a large investment of time and effort. • Identifying industry-recognized credentials may require significant research. • If the emerging industry is intertwined with the skilled labor trades, preparing low-skilled workers to be job-ready will likely require supplemental training and assistance.
… a raised awareness of the emerging industry	• Learning about the new industry and staying current requires continuous research. • Consensus on the value of specific job credentials may be lacking. • Training providers and employers are not always aware about how changing policies will affect the demand for new worker skills.
… more effective measurement of program outcomes	• If the industry is defined broadly to allow local flexbility, it may limit the comparability of reported outcome data. • Accurate counting of outcomes is difficult when the definition of the industry continues to evolve. • Training for jobs of the future may result in delayed outcomes if jobs are slow to materialize.

Source: GAO analysis of interviews with selected grantees.

Labor Has Assisted and Monitored Grantees, but Has Provided Limited Guidance on Outcome Documentation Requirements

Labor Has Provided Various Forms of Technical Assistance to Support Green Jobs Grantees

Labor has provided all green jobs grantees with technical assistance to help them implement their grant programs and comply with relevant federal laws and regulations. For example, Labor officials have hosted technical assistance webinars on topics such as financial management and how to engage employers. Labor also maintains a website for each green jobs training grant program and a green jobs community of practice on its online platform, Workforce3One. In addition, Labor has published bimonthly digests for Recovery Act grantees since January 2011 that highlight new technical assistance materials and other grant-related information. Finally, Labor has compiled and periodically updated a technical assistance guide that briefly describes and provides hyperlinks for its technical assistance resources, including webinar recordings and promising practices. Several grantees we interviewed (4 of 11) reported participating in webinars and referring to technical assistance materials posted to Workforce3One.

In addition, ETA has funded three separate studies to assess the implementation of selected green jobs programs funded by the Recovery Act. Specifically, Labor funded a 2-year implementation evaluation that examined the implementation of the three Recovery Act-funded green jobs training programs and issued both interim and final reports. [39], [40]

---

[39] The ETP, POP, and SESP grants. The evaluation also examined the implementation of the Health Care Sector and and other High Growth and Emerging Industries grant, which did not specifically target green jobs.

[40] Ted Shen, Eileen Poe-Yamagata, Alan Dodkowitz, et. al., *Green Jobs and Healthcare Implementation Study: Interim Report*, ETAOP 2012-07 (IMPAQ International: May 7, 2012). Please also see: Michael P. Kirsch, Carolyn Corea, Ted Shen, et. al., *Green Jobs and Healthcare Implementation Study Final Report*, ETAOP 2013-16 (IMPAQ International: Mar. 27, 2013).

Labor also funded an evaluation of the State Labor Market Information Improvement grants and issued a final report and additional related products in 2013.[41] Finally, Labor has funded an ongoing impact evaluation scheduled to be completed in 2016. This study was designed to test the extent to which selected grantees of one of the four green-jobs training programs overseen by ETA—Pathways Out of Poverty—improved worker outcomes by imparting skills and training valued in the labor market.[42]

To support its technical assistance efforts to grantees, Labor entered into a grant agreement with the National Governors Association, which together with two partner organizations formed a Technical Assistance Partnership (TA Partnership).[43] In conjunction with Labor officials, the TA Partnership has facilitated monthly conference calls for each grant program so grantees can learn from their peers and receive program-specific technical assistance. The TA Partnership has also compiled and updated reports that highlight promising practices grantees have implemented. Finally, the TA Partnership and Labor officials have held annual grantee conferences, which have covered various topics including strategies to retain and place program participants and the importance of nationally recognized credentials. Several (4 of 11) grantees we interviewed mentioned participating in the monthly conference calls and annual conferences and said that generally they had been helpful.

While Labor provided guidance and technical assistance on how to document eligibility for the green jobs training programs, it provided little guidance on what documentation grantees were expected to maintain regarding program outcomes, particularly with respect to job placement.

---

[41] Diane Herz, Elizabeth Laird, Angus Hague, et. al., *Investing in Labor–Market Information (LMI): Insights from the Recovery Act LMI Grants Final Report,* ETAOP 2013-05 (Mathematica Policy Research, Inc.: Jan. 15, 2013). See also: Jillian Berk, Elizabeth Laird, and Brittany English, *Investing in Labor–Market Information (LMI): A Summary of the State LMI Improvement Grants Final Report,* ETAOP 2013-06. (Mathematica Policy Research, Inc. Jan. 15, 2013). Finally, see: Elizabeth Laird, Brittany English, Jillian Berk, et.al., *Practitioner Briefs for the Evaluation of the Labor Market Information (LMI) Improvement Grants,* ETAOP 2013-17 (Mathematica Policy Research, Inc. Jan. 15, 2013).

[42] The evaluation also assesses impacts of selected grantees of another Recovery Act-funded training program, the Health Care Sector and Other High Growth and Emerging Industries grant.

[43] Specifically, the National Governors Association, Corporation for a Skilled Workforce, and Collaborative Economics form the TA Partnership.

GAO-13-555 Employment and Training

Specifically, while Labor provided guidance on how to report required performance data into its Recovery Act Database, this guidance does not specify what documentation, if any, grantees were to maintain for reported job placements, including those considered training-related. Our *Standards for Internal Control in the Federal Government* provides that internal control and all transactions and other significant events should be clearly documented and readily available for examination.[44] However, in its last green jobs report, the OIG found that nearly a quarter of reported outcomes were not supported by adequate documentation. One regional official noted that sub-grantees may not have known what documentation was required and staff in another office said that in some cases primary grantees may not have done enough to ensure that the sub-grantees they were responsible for overseeing understood documentation requirements.

While Labor officials have not issued additional guidance to GJIF grantees regarding how to document job placement and retention outcomes, they said they have taken other steps that address the OIG's recommendation to improve the quality of grantee reported performance data and utilize lessons learned from Recovery Act-funded green jobs training programs for other discretionary grant programs. First, ETA officials noted that they have formed an internal workgroup focused on improving the technical assistance provided to ETA's discretionary grantees about how to report program outcomes. This group hopes to issue recommendations in September 2013, and ETA officials believe these recommendations will help improve grant application instructions, and help ETA refine their reporting systems, among other things. Second, ETA officials told us that they had initiated a grant re-engineering project in August 2012 to identify common grant management challenges and develop strategies for addressing such challenges. For instance, the group has discussed ways to improve ETA's grant solicitation process, such as by including clearer expectations and benchmarks for performance in its solicitations for grant applications and by taking steps to ensure greater comparability of goals across grantees. Labor hopes to begin implementing the group's recommendations for new discretionary grant programs in August 2013.

---

[44] GAO, *Internal Control: Standards for Internal Control in the Federal Government*, GAO/AIMD-00-21.3.1 (Washington, D.C.: November 1999).

Labor Monitored Grantees Using a Risk-Based Approach

ETA monitors most grants, including its green jobs training grants, through a risk-based strategy that prioritizes monitoring activities based upon grantees' assessed risk-levels and availability of resources, among other factors, and is described in its Core Monitoring Guide.[45] Specifically, according to officials from all six of ETA's regional offices, ETA's federal project officers monitor grantees as part of their ongoing duties,[46] which include calling grantees to offer technical assistance. In addition, ETA's federal project officers perform quarterly desk reviews, during which they review financial reports and quarterly performance reports that grantees are required to submit.[47] For the green jobs training grants, these reports include information such as the total amount of grant funds spent, the number of participants who began or completed training, a timeline for grant activities and deliverables, grantee accomplishments, and technical assistance needs. During these quarterly reviews, federal project officers compare grantees' reported performance outcomes and spending rates to those goals set by grantees in their grant proposals. Based upon their review of each grantee's reported information, federal project officers enter information about each grantee into Labor's Grant Electronic Management System (GEMS), which assesses risk and generates a risk level for each grantee.

The GEMS assessment of each grantee's risk level is then used by Labor to develop its risk-based monitoring strategy, which involves prioritizing site visits based on grantees' assessed risk-levels and availability of resources, among other factors.[48] According to regional officials from all six offices, nearly all green jobs training grantees received at least one on-site monitoring visit, typically about halfway through the period of

---

[45] U.S. Department of Labor, Employment and Training Administration, *Core Monitoring Guide* (Washington D.C.: April 2005).

[46] Federal project officers have overall responsibility for monitoring the conduct and progress of grantees, including conducting on-site visits. Specifically, they are responsible for collaborating with the grantees—both in the planning and implementation of the program and in the evaluation of activities.

[47] Green jobs grantees were required to submit two kinds of quarterly performance reports, one that aggregated performance data and the other that described the status of program implementation in narrative form.

[48] While the risk level is primarily driven by the grantee's overall performance and financial performance, other factors also affect risk, such as the level of staff turnover at the grantee's organization, loss of key grantee personnel, or other staff issues, according to Labor officials.

performance. During these site visits, federal project officers assessed grantees' management and performance and documented any noncompliance findings and requirements for corrective action, as necessary. For example, Labor's site visit guide includes questions for federal project officers to consider about financial and performance data reporting systems and performance outcomes.

As a result of its on-site monitoring activities, Labor officials identified and required certain grantees to correct a variety of issues concerning the management of their grants. Many monitoring reports for the Recovery Act-funded green jobs training grants indicated that grantees were not on track to meet their performance outcomes. In such cases Labor required grantees to submit written corrective action plans that described what strategies they would undertake to increase project outcomes and how they would ensure that remaining funds would be used in a timely way to accomplish project objectives.

Labor officials said that grantees have made significant progress toward attaining their goals for beginning and completing training as a result of both the grantees' own efforts and ETA's technical assistance and monitoring efforts. These officials also stressed that while ETA holds grantees accountable to adhering to their grant statements of work, grantees are not contractually obligated to meet performance outcomes.[49] Unlike contracts or WIA-funded programs, which can impose sanctions for failing to meet projected targets, the accountability mechanisms for these green jobs grant programs were more limited. For example, ETA officials said that if a grantee does not achieve its placement outcomes, this can affect whether the grantee receives a period of performance extension for the current grant or, potentially, a future grant from ETA. Officials said that they had not withdrawn funding from any grantees for failing to meet performance targets for any of the four green jobs training programs. However, in some cases ETA officials decided not to grant extension requests for grantees reporting poor performance. As a result, some grant funds remained unexpended and will be returned to the Treasury, as required.

---

[49] ETA officials noted that the green jobs training programs were funded through grants and not through contracts and that this is statement is true across programs of federal assistance.

GAO-13-555 Employment and Training

In addition to insufficient progress toward targeted outcomes, the monitoring reports of the Recovery Act-funded green jobs training grantees identified other noncompliance findings, including insufficient monitoring of sub-grantees. For example, a number of monitoring reports indicated that primary grantees had not sufficiently monitored their sub-grantees. These findings are notable given that such a large percentage of grantees implemented their programs through a network of sub-grantees. Both GAO and the Department of Justice's OIG have stressed the importance of sufficient sub-recipient monitoring to the grant oversight process.[50] Other noncompliance findings included grantees lacking adequate documentation to show program participants were eligible for services or grantees having failed to follow acceptable procurement processes. According to officials from all six regional offices, federal project officers did not identify any instances of fraud, waste, or abuse during their on-site monitoring visits.

Conclusions

The Recovery Act funded multiple, substantial investments in training programs targeted to a specific emerging industry—energy efficiency and renewable energy. Most of these programs have already ended or are currently winding down, although a few of Labor's continuing programs, such as YouthBuild, have incorporated many green elements since 2009, and the Green Job Innovation Fund program is scheduled to remain active through June of 2014. Despite the sizeable investment in green jobs, the green jobs training programs have faced a number of implementation challenges and final outcomes remain uncertain, particularly regarding placement into green jobs. A number of these challenges have stemmed from the need to implement the grants quickly and simultaneously before green jobs had been defined and more had been learned about the demand for green skills. Others, such as problems with the reliability of outcome data, can be traced to management issues that have compromised Labor's ability to measure the program's success, particularly regarding placing participants into training-related employment. Specifically, because Labor did not establish clear and timely guidelines for how to document green job placement outcomes, Labor is not able to assess the extent to which the targeted

---

[50] See GAO, *Grants to State and Local Governments: An Overview of Funding Levels and Selected Challenges* GAO-12-1016 (Washington, D.C.: September 25, 2012),.24 and U.S. Department of Justice Office of the Inspector General, *Improving the Grant Management Process* (February 2009).

green jobs training programs placed participants in employment related to the training they received.

The challenges for an emerging industry such as energy efficiency and renewable energy are substantial. Uncertainty and debate still surround the question of what constitutes a green job. Under Labor's current framework, almost any job can be considered green if a link between the employee's tasks and environmental benefits can be made. Indeed, most grantee officials we interviewed said that most green jobs they have trained participants for are primarily traditional skilled-trades jobs, such as carpentry or electrical work. Many have been termed "green" because the worker has been trained to be mindful of energy use and reduce waste, or has been placed where the worker's tasks resulted in a product or service that benefited the environment, such as a light-rail construction site.

Such an approach provides certain benefits within the context of an emerging industry, in that many of the skills workers obtain can be transferred to traditional jobs in cases where local demand for green jobs falls below expectations. It also may serve to raise general worker awareness about energy efficiency and waste reduction, to the benefit of the employer or nation. Nonetheless, this emphasis on training that often takes the form of traditional skills training with an added layer of green may not fully align with the intent of the targeted training funds.

By funding several evaluations of green jobs training and labor market information programs, Labor has positioned itself to build upon lessons learned through implementing these individual programs. A fundamental consideration is whether it is prudent to implement job training programs for an emerging industry before more is known about the demand for skills and workers. Another consideration is whether it would be more or less effective for federally-funded training programs to focus on providing valuable green skills and credentials applicable on a wide variety of jobs, rather than to devote considerable attention to what is defined as a green job.

Even though Labor is scaling back its own green jobs efforts, energy efficiency and renewable energy will likely remain a national priority. Labor has established a green jobs community of practice on its online platform, Workforce3One, which, if maintained and used, can continue to facilitate information-sharing among grantees and workforce professionals regarding what green skills and credentials employers in their communities value most. In addition, the substantial investment in energy efficiency and renewable energy made through these grant programs also provides Labor an opportunity to identify broader lessons learned about the challenges and benefits associated with offering targeted training in an emerging industry, which could help inform the development of training for other emerging industries in the future. Without the benefit of such lessons learned and a continued focus on what is needed to address emerging industries, state and local workforce entities may grapple with similar challenges in the future.

Recommendations for Executive Action

To enhance Labor's ability to implement training programs in emerging industries, GAO recommends that the Secretary of Labor identify lessons learned from implementing the green jobs training programs. This could include:

- Identifying challenges and promising strategies associated with training workers for emerging industries—through both targeted grant programs and existing programs—and considering ways to improve such efforts in the future. For example, taking a more measured or multi-phased approach could allow the time necessary to better determine demand for an emerging industry and establish the partnerships needed to properly align training with available jobs.
- Taking steps to ensure training programs adequately document outcome variables, particularly for targeted programs where tracking training relatedness is of particular interest.

Agency Comments and Our Evaluation

We provided a draft of this report to the Department of Labor. Labor provided a written response (see app. IV). Labor agreed with our recommendation. Specifically, Labor's response noted that the department has already begun assessing lessons learned from the implementation of its green jobs grants. Labor also cited efforts to compile lessons learned to inform the design and implementation of future grant initiatives, including new approaches to capture program outcomes. Labor agreed that documenting outcomes is important and said it will work to provide technical assistance to ensure grantees adequately document outcomes. Finally, Labor noted the department will continue to collect information on employment outcomes and wages and will analyze these data once they are complete to provide a more definitive and final picture of the extent to which former green jobs training participants entered and retained employment.

As agreed with your offices, unless you publicly announce the contents of this report earlier, we plan no further distribution until 30 days from the report date. At that time, we will send copies to the Secretary of Labor, the Committee on Homeland Security and Governmental Affairs, the Committee on Oversight and Government Reform, and other interested parties. In addition, the report will be available at no charge on the GAO website at http://www.gao.gov.

If you or your staffs have any questions about this report, please contact me at (202) 512-7215 or sherrilla@gao.gov. Contact points for our Offices of Congressional Relations and Public Affairs may be found on the last page of this report. GAO staff who made key contributions to this report are listed in appendix V.

Andrew Sherrill
Director
Education, Workforce, and Income Security Issues

Appendix I: Objectives, Scope, and Methodology

Our objectives were to determine: (1) what is known about the objectives and coordination of the Department of Labor's (Labor) green jobs efforts, (2) what type of green jobs training grantees provided and how selected grantees aligned their training to meet employers' green jobs needs, (3) what is known about program outcomes and what challenges, if any, grantees faced in implementing their programs, and (4) what Labor has done to assist and monitor its green jobs grantees. To address these objectives, we reviewed relevant federal laws, regulations, and departmental guidance and procedures. We also created a data collection instrument and two questionnaires to obtain information from Labor officials. In addition, we analyzed data from Labor and interviewed selected grantees by phone or in person in five states—California, Illinois, Louisiana, Minnesota, and Pennsylvania—as well as Labor officials. We conducted this performance audit from May 2012 through June 2013 in accordance with generally accepted government auditing standards. Those standards require that we plan and perform the audit to obtain sufficient, appropriate evidence to provide a reasonable basis for our findings and conclusions based on our audit objectives. We believe that the evidence obtained provides a reasonable basis for our findings and conclusions based on our audit objectives.

Data Collection for Labor's Green Jobs Efforts

Our data collection strategy for obtaining information on green jobs efforts across Labor consisted of two phases.

First, we created a data collection instrument to obtain information on green jobs efforts across Labor. In the data collection instrument, we asked offices[1] at Labor to list two separate sets of efforts: (1) efforts where federal funds were appropriated or allocated specifically for green jobs activities and (2) efforts where federal funds were not specifically appropriated or allocated for green jobs activities, but where the office sought to incorporate green elements into either an existing program or ongoing activity. We distributed the data collection instrument to 14 of Labor's 28 offices: Occupational Safety and Health Administration (OSHA), Mine Safety and Health Administration (MSHA), Women's Bureau (WB), Employment and Training Administration (ETA), Veterans' Employment and Training Services (VETS), Office of the Assistant

---

[1] For the purposes of this report we refer to organizational entities within Labor as offices. These entities could include agencies, administrations, bureaus, centers, and divisions.

Secretary for Policy (OASP), Bureau of International Labor Affairs (ILAB), Bureau of Labor Statistics (BLS), Center for Faith-Based and Neighborhood Partnerships (CFBNP), Office of Federal Contract Compliance Programs (OFCCP), Wage and Hour Division (WHD), Office of Workers' Compensation Programs (OWCP), Office of Disability Employment Policy (ODEP), and the Office of Public Affairs (OPA). These 14 offices were selected based on the likelihood of their administering a green jobs effort or program. For example, we did not distribute the data collection instrument to Labor's Office of Inspector General, Office of the Solicitor, or Office of the Chief Financial Officer.

Second, we used the information we collected on the two separate sets of green jobs efforts in the data collection instruments to inform two follow-up questionnaires. For the first set of green jobs efforts, offices at Labor initially identified 16 efforts where funds were specifically appropriated or allocated for green-job related activities. For each of the 16 efforts, we sent a questionnaire by e-mail. The questionnaire focused on (1) the goals and objectives of the green jobs efforts, (2) how green jobs were defined for each of the efforts, (3) whether offices coordinated with others on these efforts, and (4) funding levels for each of the efforts. We pre-tested the questionnaire with two respondents from OSHA in December and made revisions. We then sent the questionnaires out on a rolling basis between January 16 and February 22, 2013. We determined 2 of the 16 efforts to be out of scope. Of the remaining 14 directly-funded green jobs efforts across five offices (OSHA, ETA, VETS, ILAB, and BLS), we received completed questionnaires for 13 and one partially completed questionnaire by April 3, 2013. [2] We also identified 3 additional directly-funded efforts, for a total of 17 efforts.

For the second set of green jobs efforts, offices at Labor initially identified 54 efforts where funds were not specifically appropriated or allocated for green jobs efforts, but green elements were incorporated into existing programs or ongoing activities. We identified two additional green efforts that fall under this category. We sent a brief questionnaire consisting of two questions by e-mail in an attached Microsoft Word form. The two questions included in the questionnaire were pre-tested as part of the more detailed survey mentioned above. All questionnaires were sent on

---

[2] We did not receive a completed survey for one of the efforts, but we did receive funding information for the effort that was requested in the survey in an e-mail from Labor on April 3, 2013.

January 29, 2013, or on February 22, 2013. We determined 10 of the 56
efforts to be out of scope. Of the remaining 46 efforts across six offices
(OSHA, WB, ETA, VETS, ILAB, and CFBNP), we received completed
questionnaires for all 46 efforts by March 21, 2013. Labor later identified 2
additional efforts, for a total of 48 efforts.

Because the majority of Recovery Act funding for green jobs efforts were
directed toward training programs, we focused much of our review on four
grant programs—the three training- focused green jobs training programs
funded by the Recovery Act (Energy Training Partnership grants,
Pathways Out of Poverty grants, and State Energy Sector Partnership
and Training grants) as well as the newer Green Jobs Innovation Fund.
To report on the characteristics of Labor's 103 green jobs training
grantees, we obtained data from Labor on each training-focused green
jobs grant administered by ETA. Specifically, we obtained information on
the grantee's location, organizational type, and whether or not the grantee
had sub-grantees.

Selected Grantees and Analysis of Program Outcome Data

To better understand the type of green jobs training grantees provided,
how grantees aligned their training to meet green jobs needs, and what
challenges, if any, they faced in implementing their programs, we
analyzed data from Labor and interviewed 11 out of the 103 green jobs
training grantees between August 2012 and April 2013. We conducted
site visits in four states and interviewed grantees in two additional states
by phone. We visited grantees in California, Illinois, Minnesota, and
Pennsylvania, and interviewed grantees in Connecticut and Louisiana by
phone. We selected grantees in these states because these states had a
relatively high number of Labor green jobs grant recipients, grantees in
these states received GJIF grants, and the states varied in their
geographic locations. We selected both Recovery Act- and GJIF- funded
green jobs training grantees, but emphasized GJIF-funded grantees since
unlike many of the Recovery Act programs, the GJIF program is still
active.

During each site visit we interviewed Labor's green jobs training grant
officials, training providers, local employers, and, to the extent possible,
program participants. Similarly, during our phone calls we interviewed
grant officials and in one case employers. During the interviews, we
collected information about the types of green jobs training that were
funded by Labor's green jobs training grants and the outcomes of
grantees' programs, including the impact of the training with respect to
green job placement, or otherwise. We specifically asked grantees about

any challenges they may have encountered as they developed and
implemented their program, including whether they experienced
challenges with respect to placing participants into green jobs. In addition,
we collected information on how local employers were involved in the
development of the training programs and the green job opportunities
they were able to offer program participants. We cannot generalize our
findings beyond the interviews we conducted.

To assess the reliability of Labor's training type and outcome data, we (1)
reviewed existing documentation related to the data sources, including
Labor's Office of Inspector General (OIG) reports, (2) electronically tested
the data to identify obvious problems with completeness or accuracy, and
(3) interviewed knowledgeable agency officials about the data. We
determined that the data were sufficiently reliable for limited purposes.
For example, we determined that training type data were sufficiently
reliable for purposes of reporting out on the industries for which grantees
most frequently trained participants. We included information about the
extent to which Recovery Act-funded green jobs training grantees
collectively reported meeting their enrollment, training completion, and
entered employment targets for those grantees for which final data were
available as of December 31, 2012. However, based upon the OIG's
findings, we determined that the outcome data were not sufficiently
reliable to determine the success of the programs. Finally, based upon
the OIG's findings, we determined that the data on the extent to which
grantees entered training-related employment were not reliable enough to
report, even compared to targeted levels.

Analysis of Labor's Technical Assistance and Monitoring Efforts

To describe Labor's technical assistance efforts, we reviewed technical
assistance guides and material posted to Workforce3One, interviewed
Labor officials, and discussed Labor's technical assistance with selected
grantees. To describe and assess Labor's monitoring efforts, we reviewed
its Core Monitoring guide, interviewed Labor officials in Washington, D.C.
and in each of ETA's six regional offices—Atlanta, Boston, Chicago,
Dallas, Philadelphia, and San Francisco—and obtained and reviewed
copies of Labor's monitoring reports for green jobs training grantees,
including recipients of Energy Training Partnership, Pathways Out of
Poverty, and State Energy Sector Partnership and Training grants.

Appendix II: Labor's Green Jobs Efforts since 2009 for Which Funds Were Appropriated or Allocated, by Focus Area

Focus Area: Training and supportive services		
Office	Name of effort	Reported description
ETA	Energy Training Partnership (ETP) grants	Through the Energy Training Partnership Grants, ETA awarded nearly $100 million to 25 projects. Grantees were to provide training and placement services in the energy efficiency and renewable energy industries to workers impacted by national energy and environmental policy, individuals in need of updated training related to the energy efficiency and renewable energy industries, and unemployed workers. Grantees were required to partner with labor organizations, employers and workforce investment boards. Grant awards ranged from approximately $1.4 to $5 million.
ETA	Pathways Out of Poverty (POP) grants	In total, Pathways Out of Poverty grantees received approximately $150 million in Recovery Act funds. The grant aimed to help targeted populations find pathways out of poverty through employment in energy efficiency and renewable energy industries. Grants ranged from approximately $2 million to $8 million and were awarded to eight national nonprofit organizations with local affiliates and to 30 local public organizations or private nonprofit organizations.
ETA	State Energy Sector Partnership and Training (SESP) grants	Through SESP, ETA awarded nearly $190 million to state workforce investment boards in partnership with state workforce agencies. The grants were designed to provide training, job placement, and related activities that reflect a comprehensive statewide energy sector strategy including the governor's overall workforce vision, state energy policies, and training activities that lead to employment in targeted industry sectors. ETA made 34 awards that ranged from approximately $2 to $6 million each.
ETA	Green Jobs Innovation Fund (GJIF)	The Green Jobs Innovation Fund was authorized under the Workforce Investment Act to help workers receive job training in green industry sectors and occupations and access green career pathways. In total, $38 million in grant funds were awarded to six organizations with networks of local affiliates to develop green jobs training programs. These programs were required to incorporate green career pathways either by forging linkages between Registered Apprenticeship and pre-apprenticeship programs or by integrating the delivery of technical and basic skills training through community-based partnerships.
ETA	Job Corps	Job Corps is a residential job training program for at-risk youth. The Job Corps program aims to teach participants the skills they need to secure a meaningful job, continue their education, and be independent. Job Corps has instituted a number of measures in recent years to "green" its job training programs and facilities. Recovery Act funding was used to incorporate "green" training elements into the automotive, advanced manufacturing, and construction trades at Job Corps centers nationwide and to pilot three new "green" training programs at selected Job Corps centers: Solar Panel Installation, Weatherization, and SmartGrid technology.
OSHA	Susan Harwood Training Grant Program	Targeted topic training grant in which applicants propose training based on the occupational safety and health topics chosen by OSHA. Alternative Energy Industry Hazards and Green Jobs Industry Hazards were included as topics in FY 2009 and FY 2010, respectively.

Focus Area: Training and supportive services		
Office	Name of effort	Reported description
VETS	Veterans' Workforce Investment Program (VWIP)	VWIP supports veterans' employment and training services to help eligible veterans reintegrate into meaningful employment and to stimulate the development of effective and targeted service delivery systems. In FYs 2009 and 2010, project proposals received priority consideration if they supported "Green Energy Jobs" and proposed clear strategies for training and employment in the renewable energy economy.

Focus Area: Data collection and reporting		
Office	Name of effort	Reported description
ETA	State Labor Market Information Improvement (SLMII) grants	ETA awarded approximately $48.8 million in State Labor Market Information Improvement Grants to support the research and analysis of labor market data to assess economic activity in energy efficiency and renewable energy industries and identify occupations within those industries. Grant activities included collecting and disseminating labor market information, enhancing strategies to connect job seekers to green job banks, and helping ensure that workers find employment after completing training. ETA awarded 30 grants of between $763,000 and $4 million.
BLS	Green Goods and Services (GGS) program	This is a survey-based program, covering 120,000 business establishments, which provides a measure of national and state employment in industries that produce goods or provide services that benefit the environment.
BLS	Occupational Employment and Wages in Green Goods and Services (GGS-OCC) program	This program provides occupational employment and wage information for businesses that produce green goods and services.
BLS	Green Technologies and Practices (GTP) survey	This is a special survey of business establishments designed to collect data on establishments' use of green technologies and practices and the occupations of workers who spend more than half of their time involved in green technologies and practices.
BLS	Employment Projections program	Green Career Information staff within the Employment Projections program produces career information on green jobs including wages, expected job prospects, what workers do on the job, working conditions, and necessary education, training, and credentials.

Focus Area: Technical assistance		
Office	Name of effort	Reported description
ETA	Occupational Information Network (O*NET)	Information that O*NET provided was used to support all Recovery Act green jobs grantees who were doing green jobs data collection and training in the states. These Recovery Act funds to O*NET were for the specific purpose of focusing occupational research and data collection on green jobs on an accelerated pace.
ETA	Technical Assistance	The Technical Assistance Partnership led by the National Governor's Association supported Recovery Act-funded green jobs grantees.

Appendix II: Labor's Green Jobs Efforts since
2009 for Which Funds Were Appropriated or
Allocated, by Focus Area

Focus Area: Other - Capacity building, administrative expenses, information materials, partnerships		
Office	Name of effort	Reported description
ETA	Green Capacity Building Grants (GCBG)	In total, ETA awarded $5 million in Recovery Act funds to training programs already funded by the Department of Labor to build their capacity to provide training in the energy efficiency and renewable energy industries. ETA awarded 62 of these grants, with awards ranging from $50,000 to $100,000.
ETA	Administrative Expenses	ETA used $5 million of the $500 million authorized for the Recovery Act green jobs grants for administrative expenses (salaries and expenses). This does not include any funds that were retained for technical assistance for these grants. Administrative expenses were in part used to fund three separate evaluations of Recovery Act green jobs programs: (1) a Labor Market Information evaluation, (2) a green jobs and health care implementation report, and (3) a 5-year impact evaluation.
OSHA	Nanomaterials Safe Practice and Handling Guidelines	This guidance was funded by the Recovery Act and is a guidance document for R&D workers and employers in the nanotechnology field.
ILAB	Trilateral Roundtable: The Employment Dimension of the Transition to a Green Economy (February 3-4, 2011)	The U.S. Department of Labor, Human Resources and Skills Development Canada and the European Commission brought together U.S., Canadian, and European experts representing governments, trade unions, industry, and nongovernmental organizations to discuss the transition to the green economy. Discussions focused on defining and measuring green jobs, establishing effective green jobs partnerships, designing green skills development and training, ensuring green jobs serve as a pathway out of poverty, and examining the quality of green jobs, as well as the sustainability of green jobs investments by governments.

Source: Responses provided by Labor.

Focus Area: Information materials		
Office	Name of effort	Reported description
ETA	Office of Apprenticeship (OA)	In June 2009, Labor/ETA/OA published a report entitled, "The Greening of Registered Apprenticeship: An Environmental Scan of the Impact of Green Jobs on Registered Apprenticeship and Implications for Workforce Development." More recently, as part of the 75th Anniversary of the National Apprenticeship Act in 2012, OA put out a call to sponsors across the county to collect Registered Apprenticeship Innovators or Trailblazers. This process identified a number of innovative programs across the country, including several specific examples of apprenticeship programs with a focus on green efforts.
ILAB	OECD Working Party on Employment; April 11, 2012	Labor officials participated in a technical review of economic research presented in "What Green Growth Means for Workers and Labour Market Policies: An Initial Assessment." Subsequently the paper appeared as Chapter 4 in the 2012 OECD Employment Outlook.
OSHA	Green Job Hazards Web-site	An OSHA website providing green job safety information on specific green jobs, such as green roofing, waste management, wind energy, recycling, weatherization, and geothermal industries.
OSHA	Workforce Guidelines for Home Energy Upgrades	Provided safety information for weatherization jobs in collaboration with Department of Energy, Environmental Protection Agency, and National Institute for Occupational Safety and Health (NIOSH)
OSHA	EPA's Healthy Indoor Environment Protocols for Home Energy Upgrades	OSHA worked with EPA in the publication of this guidance which identifies critical indoor environmental quality risks and worker assessment protocols, and provides guidance to address these issues.
OSHA	Green and Clean: How Hospitals Can Protect Patients and Workers by Using Earth-Friendly and Sustainable Products/Practices	Through OSHA and The Joint Commission and Joint Commission Resources (JCR) Alliance, JCR developed an article that discusses the importance of adopting sustainable products and practices for cleaning, sanitizing, and disinfecting healthcare facilities. The article also provides requirements for selecting green cleaning products (January 2013).
WB	Why Green is Your Color, Manual	Publishing of a manual: Why Green Is Your Color: A Woman's Guide to a Sustainable Career. Designed to assist women with job training and career development.
WB	Teleconference Calls and Fact Sheets	A series of teleconferences for workforce practitioners about how to connect women with green jobs. A fact sheet accompanied each teleconference.

**Appendix III: Labor's Green Jobs Efforts since
2009 for Which Funds Were Not Appropriated
or Allocated, by Focus Area**

Focus Area: Partnerships		
Office	**Name of effort**	**Reported description**
CFBNP	Facilitated a partnership between OSHA regional office and green jobs grantee	In May 2010, the Deputy Director of CFBNP facilitated a partnership between OSHA's Cincinnati office and East End Community Services in Dayton, OH – a Pathways Out of Poverty sub-grantee seeking a training module on safe handling of asbestos and lead removal as part of a green jobs training program.
ETA	Interagency working groups (with Energy, Education, and HUD)	Interagency working groups related to clean energy and green jobs in which Labor works with the U.S. Departments of Education, Energy, and Housing and Urban Development
ILAB	March 21, 2012 Anniversary Paper from the 2011 Trilateral Roundtable on the Transition to a Green Economy	The U.S. Department of Labor, Human Resources and Skills Development Canada and the European Commission each contributed two updates on promising practices or strategies that were first explored at the Roundtable
ILAB	2012 G20 Labor and Employment Ministers' meeting, May 17-18, 2012	International labor and employment ministers met to discuss employment issues, including green jobs and high youth unemployment rates
ILAB	Participated in OECD's Employment, Labor and Social Affairs Committee meeting that discussed a green jobs project	Labor officials participated in the October 13-14, 2011 ELSAC meeting in Paris, France. One topic discussed at the meeting was the OECD's green jobs project.
ILAB	Rio+20 Conference on Sustainable Development input	Labor staff articulated labor and employment priorities to the U.S. interagency for inclusion in U.S. government positions for Rio+20, including for the U.S. position paper and during negotiations of the Rio outcome document.
ILAB	International Labor Organization Governing Body	Labor staff participated in International Labor Organization Governing Body discussions on green jobs and sustainable development
ILAB	Asia-Pacific Economic Cooperation Symposium on Human Capital Policies for Green Growth and Employment	The two-day Symposium convened experts from 16 Asia-Pacific Economic Cooperation member economies and international organizations to discuss sustainable economic development policies. The event was hosted by the Department of Education, in partnership with Labor.
ILAB	US-Brazil Memorandum of Understanding on Labor Cooperation (March 20-21, 2012)	U.S. Secretary of Labor and her counterpart from Brazil signed a Memorandum of Understanding on Labor Cooperation in May 2012. The memorandum highlights cooperation in the area of green jobs.
ILAB	Information exchange with officials from Brazil's Ministry of Environmental Affairs about U.S. Labor's Green Jobs Initiatives	The Women's Bureau Director led a Labor delegation meeting with officials from Brazil's Ministry of Environmental Affairs at U.S. EPA about the definition of green jobs, and initiatives in both countries.
ILAB	Inter-American Conference of Ministers of Labor, of the Organization of American States	The October 2012 conference working group meetings considered green jobs in follow-up to the XVII IACML Declaration and Plan of Action adopted by the ministers of labor of the Americas in November 2011. The Plan of Action called for specific follow-up actions related to green jobs including, inter-alia, in-depth exchange of best practices in the region.
ILAB	African Growth and Opportunity Act's African Women Entrepreneur Program Briefing	DOL officials met with 47 women leaders from Sub-Saharan Africa under the African Growth and Opportunity Act's African Women Entrepreneur Program, sharing best practices, perspectives and strategies to train and employ women in green jobs.
OSHA	Federal Workgroup on Spray Polyurethane Foam	Federal workgroup (EPA, OSHA, NIOSH, CPSC) working with industry groups (ACC, CPI, SPFI) on environmental, occupational, and consumer health and safety issues with the use of spray polyurethane foam weatherization products

Appendix III: Labor's Green Jobs Efforts since
2009 for Which Funds Were Not Appropriated
or Allocated, by Focus Area

Focus Area: Partnerships		
Office	Name of effort	Reported description
OSHA	OSHA/American Wind Energy Association Alliance	Presentations by Deputy Assistant Secretary of Labor for Occupational Safety and Health to general session, sharing of knowledge, development of informational products and participation in quarterly meetings.
OSHA	Recovery through Retrofit: Meeting	OSHA and Labor participated in an interagency Recovery through Retrofit Working Group comprised of over 80 technical staff members from the Departments of Energy, Housing and Urban Development, and Labor; Environmental Protection Agency; ,and USD that drafted standards for workers who will be involved in retrofitting homes to make them more energy efficient. The group met in Denver for a 3 days and a follow-up meeting was held in Washington D.C. This is the Vice President's initiative. As a part of the working group, OSHA provided technical advice and input in the worker protection aspects of the standards that were drafted.
OSHA	National Alliance with the Professional Landcare Network (PLANET)	One of the goals of this Alliance is to participate in PLANET's Green Industry Conference
Focus Area: Publicity and outreach		
Office	Name of effort	Reported description
CFBNP	Secretary of Labor and CFBNP Hold Green Jobs Discussion with Philanthropic Leaders	On December 1, 2010, Secretary of Labor and Assistant Secretary for Employment and Training met with leaders from several national foundations to discuss significant investments in green jobs programs, as well as effective strategies that create employment and advancement opportunities for low-income populations in the green job industry.
CFBNP	Publicity of RecycleForce green jobs program for ex-offenders	In 2012, the Director of CFBNP wrote a blog for Fatherhood.gov about an Employment and Training Administration's grantee RecycleForce that provides green jobs to ex-offenders.
ETA	Job Train's "Earth Day Every Day Campaign"	Held the week of April 19th-23rd, 2010, the campaign was designed "to raise environmental awareness among students and staff and serve as friendly reminders to be more energy efficient."
ILAB	Briefing for Chinese Embassy official	Labor staff briefed an official from the Chinese Embassy on Labor green jobs initiatives.
ILAB	Briefing for Confederation of Venezuelan Labor Washington, DC liaison	Labor staff briefed the liaison on Labor green jobs efforts.
OSHA	Small Business Forum: "Green Jobs: Safety & Health Outlook for Workers and Small Employers"	A forum on OSHA's green jobs efforts and workplace hazards associated with green jobs.
OSHA	Presentation at the Center for Polyurethane Industry Annual Conference	Presentation – "What You Need to Know About the Safe Use of Spray Polyurethane Foam (SPF) Briefing on Spray Polyurethane Foam"
OSHA	Participate in NIOSH Going Green Workshop	OSHA Team attended as participating partner and Assistant Secretary spoke.
OSHA	US/EU Conference Brussels	OSHA co-chaired the topic, "OSH in Green Economy" for the conference on behalf of the United States. OSHA led the discussions and wrote the accompanying white paper.
OSHA	Green Jobs, Good Jobs National Conference	OSHA senior staff made presentations at conference on hazards of green jobs.

Appendix III: Labor's Green Jobs Efforts since
2009 for Which Funds Were Not Appropriated
or Allocated, by Focus Area

Focus Area: Publicity and outreach		
Office	Name of effort	Reported description
OSHA	Green Jobs, Good Jobs, Regional Conferences	OSHA personnel made presentations in Atlanta, GA; Los Angeles, CA; Philadelphia, PA; and Detroit, MI.
OSHA	Trilateral Roundtable: With Canada and European Commission	OSHA participated in: The Employment Dimension of the Transition to a Green Economy". The event brought together experts from government, trade unions, industry, and other stakeholders to exchange information, best practices, and ideas on preparing workers and employers to meet the increasingly complex skill demands of this transition. OSHA made a presentation on Green Jobs hazards.
OSHA	OSHA Alliance Program Construction Roundtable	Roundtable has received presentations from CPWR, NIOSH and Department of Commerce on green jobs within the construction industry.
OSHA	CleanMed Conference on Worker Safety, Patient Safety, Environmental Safety	First Annual Research Exchange on Advancing Patient, Worker and Environmental Safety and Sustainability in the Health Care Sector. OSHA presentation on focus on green jobs in relation to the healthcare industry. The audience was mainly healthcare workers, employers and researchers.
OSHA	OSHA – NIOSH Infosheet & Posters: Protecting Workers Who Use Cleaning Chemical	Provides information to employers on practices to help keep workers safe when working with cleaning chemicals, including green cleaning products. The posters are available in English, Chinese, Tagalog and Spanish. The poster includes a section devoted to Green Cleaners.
OSHA	Presentation at American Industrial Hygiene Conference & Exposition	Topic: Making Green Jobs Good Jobs – We All Want To, So What is OSHA Doing to Make it Happen?
WB	Women and Green Jobs Roundtables	Discussions at over 30 U.S. locations involving business and community leaders regarding emerging employment opportunities in green job fields.
WB	Why Green is Your Color, outreach materials	Posters, mobile marketing displays, postcards, flash drives.
Focus Area: Technical assistance		
Office	Name of effort	Reported description
ETA	Green Jobs Community of Practice (CoP) on Workforce3One	ETA designed the Green jobs CoP to serve as a platform for workforce professionals and green job thought leaders to discuss and share promising practices, to create partnerships for green job workforce solutions, and to leverage Recovery Act investments. Specifically, the Green Jobs CoP was designed to provide an interactive platform for providing technical assistance through webinars, discussion boards, blogs and other online resources to workforce professionals, particularly those at the state and workforce investment board levels as well as green jobs grantees (including recipients of upcoming Solicitation for Grant Applications).
Focus Area: Training and supportive services		
Office	Name of effort	Reported description
ETA	YouthBuild	The YouthBuild program targets out-of-school youth ages 16 to 24 and provides them with an alternative education pathway to a high school diploma or GED. Most YouthBuild programs have incorporated green building into their construction training. As part of this training, participants learn about environmental issues that affect their communities and how they can provide leadership in this area.
OSHA	Blue-Green Alliance Conference	Attended the Blue-Green Alliance conference

Appendix III: Labor's Green Jobs Efforts since
2009 for Which Funds Were Not Appropriated
or Allocated, by Focus Area

Focus Area: Training and supportive services		
Office	Name of effort	Reported description
VETS	Homeless Veterans' Reintegration Program	The purpose of this program is to expedite the reintegration of homeless veterans into the labor force. These grants are intended to address two objectives: to provide services to assist in reintegrating homeless veterans into meaningful employment within the labor force, and to stimulate the development of effective service delivery systems that will address the complex problems facing homeless veterans. The programs' technical assistance guide refers to collecting data on green jobs participants.
WB	Why Green is Your Color, Web-based training	Web-based training to help women find and succeed in green jobs.
WB	Green Jobs for Women Pilot Training Projects	Pilot training projects designed to prepare women to enter high-growth, high-demand green jobs.

Source: Responses provided by Labor.

Appendix IV: Comments from the Department of Labor

U.S. Department of Labor

Assistant Secretary for
Employment and Training
Washington, D.C. 20210

JUN 1 2 2013

Mr. Andrew Sherrill
Director
Education, Workforce, and Income Security Issues
U.S. Government Accountability Office
441 G. Street, N.W.
Washington, D.C. 20548

Dear Mr. Sherrill:

On behalf of the U.S. Department of Labor (DOL), I want to thank you for the opportunity to review and comment on the Government Accountability Office's (GAO) draft report entitled: *Labor's Green Jobs Efforts Highlight Challenges of Targeted Training Programs for Emerging Industries* (GAO-13-555).

The GAO report recommends the following:

To enhance Labor's ability to implement training programs in emerging industries, GAO recommends that the Secretary of Labor identify lessons learned from implementing the green jobs training programs. This could include:

- *Identifying challenges and promising strategies associated with training workers for emerging industries–through both targeted grant programs and existing programs–and considering ways to improve such efforts in the future. For example, taking a more measured or multi-phased approach could allow the time necessary to better determine demand for an emerging industry and establish the partnerships needed to properly align training with available jobs.*
- *Taking steps to ensure training programs adequately document outcome variables, particularly for targeted populations where tracking training relatedness is of particular interest.*

The Department agrees with this recommendation and has already begun assessing lessons learned from the initial implementation of its green jobs grants. An important element of the comprehensive technical assistance plan supporting these grants has been to document practices, in areas such as grants management, employer engagement, training, and participant follow-up, throughout the grant period, and to compile a listing of lessons learned upon completion of the grants in June, 2013 to inform the design and implementation of future grant initiatives, including new approaches to capture program outcomes.

An example of how DOL has already identified promising strategies to shape a grant solicitation is the development of the Green Jobs Innovation Fund (GJIF) initiative in 2011, which was based on lessons learned from the Recovery Act grants. During the implementation of the Recovery Act grants, DOL reviewed research findings and feedback from grantees, employers, industry, and other key stakeholders, to identify work-based training models, such as Registered

Apprenticeship and On-the-Job Training, as valuable learning strategies because they help
participants acquire the skills employers need while participants earn wages. In addition, the
Recovery Act grants have reinforced, that for many, the need to upgrade basic skills as well as
acquire new occupational skills is critical to job placement. DOL is incorporating these lessons
by funding GJIF grantees to implement green jobs training programs that develop stronger
linkages with Registered Apprenticeship and pre-apprenticeship programs and/or integrate basic
skills and occupational training programs in partnership with community-based organizations.
DOL also continues to incorporate work-based learning opportunities into later grant
solicitations.

DOL agrees that documenting outcomes is important and will work to continue to provide
technical assistance to ensure that grantees adequately document outcomes achieved, with a
focus on the Department's three adult common performance outcomes of employment, job
retention, and average earnings. DOL also agrees that collecting information on training-related
employment outcome variables helps to inform program management and continuous
improvement activities as well as to illustrate program success. We also believe that the ultimate
success of the programs should be measured by the three employment-related outcome measures
which the Department currently uses for its adult job training and employment programs.

As the report acknowledges, DOL will continue to collect additional information on employment
outcomes and wages using state unemployment insurance (UI) wage record data for all
participants of the green jobs training grants, which is available to DOL nine months after
participants exit the program. Preliminary results based on UI wage records as of December 31,
2012, for participants who were unemployed at entry and have exited green jobs programs show
a 52 percent employment rate. For those who found employment, 83 percent retained
employment for six-months after completing a green jobs training program. They earned
average earnings of about $25,000 for a six-month period after program completion. After the
grants close, and longer-term UI wage record data become available, the Employment Training
Administration will assess employment outcomes using complete UI wage data to provide a
more definitive and final picture of the extent to which former green jobs training participants
entered and retained employment.

Again, thank you for the opportunity to review the draft report. If you would like additional
information, please do not hesitate to call me at (202) 693-2700.

Sincerely,

Gerri Fiala
Acting Assistant Secretary

Appendix V: GAO Contact and Staff Acknowledgments

GAO Contact	Andrew Sherrill, (202) 512-7215 or sherrilla@gao.gov
Staff Acknowledgments	In addition to the contact named above, Laura Heald, Assistant Director; Amy Buck, Meredith Moore, and David Perkins made significant contributions to all phases of the work. Also contributing to this report were James Bennett, David Chrisinger, Stanley Czerwinski, Beryl Davis, Andrea Dawson, Peter Del Toro, Alexander Galuten, Kathy Leslie, Sheila McCoy, Kim McGatlin, Jean McSween, Rhiannon Patterson, Karla Springer, Vanessa Taylor, and Mark Ward.

Related GAO Products

Grants to State and Local Governments: An Overview of Funding Levels and Selected Challenges. GAO-12-1016. Washington, D.C.: September 25, 2012.

Renewable Energy: Federal Agencies Implement Hundreds of Initiatives. GAO-12-260. Washington, D.C.: February 27, 2012.

Workforce Investment Act: Innovative Collaborations between Workforce Boards and Employers Helped Meet Local Needs. GAO-12-97. Washington, D.C.: January 19, 2012.

Climate Change: Improvements Needed to Clarify National Priorities and Better Align Them with Federal Funding Decisions. GAO-11-317. Washington, D.C.: May 20, 2011.

Recovery Act: Energy Efficiency and Conservation Block Grant Recipients Face Challenges Meeting Legislative and Program Goals and Requirements. GAO-11-379. Washington, D.C.: April 7, 2011.

Multiple Employment and Training Programs: Providing Information on Colocating Services and Consolidating Administrative Structures Could Promote Efficiencies. GAO-11-92. Washington, D.C.: January 13, 2011.

Recovery Act: States' and Localities' Uses of Funds and Actions Needed to Address Implementation Challenges and Bolster Accountability. GAO-10-604. Washington, D.C.: May 26, 2010.

Recovery Act: Funds Continue to Provide Fiscal Relief to States and Localities, While Accountability and Reporting Challenges Need to Be Fully Addressed. GAO-09-1016. Washington, D.C.: September 23, 2009.

Employment and Training Program Grants: Evaluating Impact and Enhancing Monitoring Would Improve Accountability. GAO-08-486. Washington, D.C.: May 7, 2008.

Workforce Investment Act: Additional Actions Would Improve the Workforce System. GAO-07-1061T. Washington, D.C.: June 28, 2007.

Workforce Investment Act: Employers Found One-Stop Centers Useful in Hiring Low-Skilled Workers; Performance Information Could Help Gauge Employer Involvement. GAO-07-167. Washington, D.C.: December 22, 2006.

Workforce Investment Act: Substantial Funds Are Used for Training, but Little Is Known Nationally about Training Outcomes. GAO-05-650. Washington, D.C.: June 29, 2005.

Workforce Investment Act: Employers Are Aware of, Using, and Satisfied with One-Stop Services, but More Data Could Help Labor Better Address Employers' Needs. GAO-05-259. Washington, D.C.: February 18, 2005.

Workforce Investment Act: States and Local Areas Have Developed Strategies to Assess Performance, but Labor Could Do More to Help. GAO-04-657. Washington, D.C.: June 1, 2004.

Workforce Investment Act: One-Stop Centers Implemented Strategies to Strengthen Services and Partnerships, but More Research and Information Sharing Is Needed. GAO-03-725. Washington, D.C.: June 18, 2003.

Internal Control: Standards for Internal Control in the Federal Government, GAO/AIMD-00-21.3.1. Washington, D.C.: November 1999.